Presented To:

_____

From:

_____

Date:

THE ART OF
INFLUENCE

YOUR **COMPETITIVE** EDGE

JIM STOVALL
& RAY H. HULL, PhD

SOUND WISDOM
P.O. Box 310
Shippensburg, PA 17257-0310

For more information on publishing and distribution rights, call 717-530-2122 or info@soundwisdom.com

Quantity Sales. Special discounts are available on quantity purchases by corporations, associations, and others. For details, contact the Sales Department at Sound Wisdom.

While efforts have been made to verify information contained in this publication, neither the author nor the publisher assumes any responsibility for errors, inaccuracies, or omissions.

While this publication is chock-full of useful, practical information, it is not intended to be legal or accounting advice. All readers are advised to seek competent lawyers and accountants to follow laws and regulations that may apply to specific situations.

The reader of this publication assumes responsibility for the use of the information. The author and publisher assume no responsibility or liability whatsoever on the behalf of the reader of this publication.

ISBN 13 HC: 978-1-64095-032-0
ISBN 13 TP: 978-1-64095-060-3
ISBN 13 eBook: 978-1-64095-033-7

For Worldwide Distribution, Printed in the U.S.A.

Cover/Jacket designer Eileen Rockwell
Interior design by Terry Clifton

1 2 3 4 5 6 7 8 / 21 20 19 18

CONTENTS

CHAPTER ONE

UNDERSTANDING INFLUENCE

Influence is everywhere all the time whether we realize it or not.
—JIM STOVALL

Among the billions of people who inhabit the earth today, there are very few aspects of life that touch us all, but without exception, we are all influenced by outside forces just as we influence the world around us. It is impossible to avoid influencing others or being influenced by them. Even those whom we treat indifferently are influenced by our indifference just as we are influenced by those who may totally ignore us; therefore, it is incumbent upon us to understand influence and become proactive in how we influence others and allow others to influence us.

This book is my fourth literary collaboration with Dr. Ray Hull. Previously, we have combined our efforts in *The Art of Communication*, *The Art of Presentation*, and *The Art of Learning and Self-Development*. My work with Dr. Hull is a product of influence. A colleague at the U.S. Department of Education, Jo Ann McCann, went out of her way to introduce me to Ray and challenge me to consider how we might combine our efforts.

At first glance, it would seem that a blind guy like me and an eminent expert in the field of audiology like Dr. Hull would have very little, if anything, in common, but Jo Ann's influence on both of us birthed a creative output that would not have been possible by Dr. Hull or myself individually.

This book was originally envisioned as a project that would focus on leadership, but due to the creative influence of Dave Wildasin at my publisher, Sound Wisdom, I came to understand how many books had already been written about leadership, and while important, leadership is dwarfed by the overarching concept of influence. All leaders are influencers, but not all influencers are leaders in the traditional sense. I remain grateful to Dave Wildasin for influencing me and my readers through this book.

Influence impacts every area of our lives. If you think of people who are antisocial or involved with the counterculture, you might assume they are not influenced by the world around them, but after further reflection, it becomes inescapable that even these people who have chosen to be outside the norm are impacted by the very norm they reject. To be the opposite of something, you must first identify it, then move in the other direction.

One of the best sales trainers I know is fond of saying, "You cannot not decide." This reminds us that delaying, ignoring, or avoiding a decision is a decision. An elected representative charged with the responsibility of voting on behalf of his or her constituency who abstains during a critical vote has made an influential decision that will impact the outcome of the ruling.

When I was growing up in Tulsa, Oklahoma, our family attended the First Baptist Church. I was greatly influenced by lessons I learned there and the pastor, Dr. Warren Hultgren. Listening to Dr. Hultgren speak each Sunday influenced me to become a corporate, convention, and arena speaker myself. His style of communicating and presenting was infectious. He drew people toward his message instead of thrusting it on them. Dr. Hultgren and I became great friends, and he influenced me throughout his retirement years and up to the time of his death. In many ways, he still influences me today.

While I don't attend that church very often today due to my travel schedule surrounding speaking engagements as well as book and movie projects, whenever I'm home, I listen to the Sunday services that are broadcast on the radio. A gentleman I greatly respect named Deron Spoo is now the pastor, and I will never forget a point he made within one of his Sunday messages saying, "There is no neutral influence."

That simple quote involves a depth of wisdom that it is difficult to fully grasp. If we realize and accept the fact that everything we do, everything we say, and everything we think will influence us and everyone around us, we are compelled to live our lives in a different way.

Whether we're examining our personal or professional lives, our progress often seems random and chaotic. We seem to be buffeted about like an autumn leaf in the wind with little or no control of ourselves or the things around us. But then, from time to time, we achieve a victorious milestone or suffer a devastating defeat. When we look back over our lives from these high or low vantage points, we discover that what seemed like random chaos was actually influential forces impacting us that culminated in our success or failure.

If our success, failure, or very existence is dependent upon these outside influences, it is incumbent on us to take control of our destiny and choose how we will be influenced and how we will influence others. Often, powerful influences begin as tiny seeds that, years later, can emerge as irresistible forces or immovable objects that shape who we are and what we do.

Neonatal experts have discovered that we are influenced by motion, sounds, and other stimuli even when we're in the womb, and if you've ever been in the home of a family expecting a baby, you will certainly understand that the child has a great influence on people and things around it before it's even born.

I was born my parents' third child, but my older brother and sister both died at a very young age. I never knew my brother as he passed away from a lung disorder before I was born, and my sister died of a form of leukemia when I was a small child. It's difficult for me to separate what I remember of my sister from the family stories and photos of her that were shared with me later. Although I was an only child until my younger brother came along when I was in kindergarten, the influence of my older brother and sister was felt throughout my formative years and to this very day.

I have written over 40 books, and thankfully, they have all been well received, but by far my most successful title is a novel I wrote entitled *The Ultimate Gift*, which was made into a movie with Twentieth Century Fox. If you've seen that film and experienced the powerful performance Abigail Breslin gave as the character Emily, you will understand that I was influenced greatly by my sister as I wrote about a young girl named Emily dying from leukemia.

Our influence precedes our birth and continues beyond our death. The popular term *legacy* is nothing more than the ongoing influence our lives have on the world even after we have passed away.

We have a tendency to think of events in our lives as either good or bad. We win the lottery and believe that it is good, or we suffer a financial or career setback and consider it to be bad. In reality, we can choose how events influence us. For everyone devastated by a tragic occurrence in their life, I can show you someone else experiencing the same tragedy who uses it as a springboard toward their goals and their eventual success.

Many events that would be considered positive can turn out to have a negative influence on us. Lottery winners file for bankruptcy within a few years of winning their prize at a rate higher than the general public. Getting a promotion or a better job might seem to be a positive influence on the surface but not if it keeps us from starting our own business or moving toward the job of our dreams.

As a young man, I had no greater ambition in life than to be an All-American football player, then move on to make my living in the NFL. The coaches, scouts, and experts that evaluate players assured me that I had the size, speed, and talent to reach my goal. So, I felt the course of my life was set, and I didn't worry about anything else such as studying or preparing for an alternative career.

Then one year during a routine physical exam to go play another season of football, I was confronted with one of the greatest influences in my life.

I remember going through that routine physical which was simply the standard operating procedure before the football season began. The doctors poke you, prod you, measure you, and weigh you, and everything seemed to be going smoothly as it had in previous years until one of the doctors shined a light in my right eye and then feverishly wrote something in my chart.

He picked up a phone and called for another doctor who rushed into the room and shined his light in both my eyes, then nodded to the first doctor and left. Eventually, a third doctor came into the room and ran several other tests that were quite involved and had not been a part of my previous football physical examinations.

Finally, the three doctors took me down a long hall and sat me down at a conference table where they told me they weren't sure why or when but were certain that I was going to be totally blind, and there was nothing they could do about it.

My whole world seemed to stop in that one moment. My plans of being an All-American and NFL player were gone in the proverbial and literal blink of an eye.

At this writing, that was more than 40 years ago, and living my life as a blind person influences me every day, but it might surprise you to know that the influence has been and continues to be overwhelmingly positive. We don't always have a choice about what happens to us, but we can always choose what we're going to do about it and how we are going to allow it to influence us.

Realizing my football career was over, I enrolled in a local college—desperately trying to make sense of my looming blindness and grasping for a new direction regarding what I was going to do with the rest of my life. As I began attending classes that fall, it quickly became apparent to me that my previous academic apathy and lack of effort had left me woefully behind my classmates. On top of the scholastic challenges, the football doctors were proven right when my eyesight began to fade, and I found myself unable to read and struggling to get around on my own.

I did what I thought was the only logical, sensible thing to do and dropped out of college. Then, one of the greatest influences in my life began to pursue me with a passion.

I had met Dr. Herald Paul in one of the few classes I had attended before dropping out of college. Dr. Paul taught humanities, and I didn't know at that time that he was considered one of the world's leading experts in his field and had received the highest honors both as a scholar and an educator.

I took a job as a construction worker, which was the only thing I knew how to do at that time. I had no particular skills or talent, but I was bigger and stronger than most of the other guys on the job, so I shoveled concrete, unloaded steel, or did whatever other difficult, hot, and nasty jobs needed to be done on the construction site.

Dr. Paul got in the habit of showing up wherever I was working around the lunch hour. It is ironic and comical today to look back on that eminent scholar and renowned educator, wearing his immaculate suit while sitting on a pile of boards with me, eating a sack lunch. Without overtly prodding or nagging me, Dr. Paul encouraged me to consider returning to college and resuming my education. Not only did Dr. Paul influence me, but his noontime appearances began to have an influence on the other construction workers on the job to the point where they virtually forced me to quit my construction job and re-enroll in college.

That next fall, I was back in the same classes, with less vision than I'd had the year before and another year removed from my weak academic preparations, but I had one thing going for me which was the influence of Dr. Herald Paul.

The university I attended had never had a blind or visually impaired student before, so Dr. Paul knocked on doors, kicked others down, and created a system for me to receive my education. One of the provisions that Dr. Paul made was to arrange for other students to read my textbooks to me. The greatest influence in my life appeared in the form of one of those college students tasked with reading my textbooks aloud to me.

The moment I met Crystal, I knew I wouldn't need any other readers because somehow I understood I had just met the most significant and influential person in my life. At this writing, we have been married 37 years, and Crystal continues to be the greatest factor in my success.

With Dr. Paul clearing the way and with Crystal's support, I discovered that I was a good student, and I actually had a level of intelligence I had not imagined.

Four years later, I graduated second in our class, and it probably won't surprise you to learn that Crystal graduated first. I am absolutely convinced that without losing my sight, I would have never been an adequate student or even finished college—much less someone who graduated with honors. I came to understand that disappointments and even disabilities are powerless in the face of positive influences.

Near the end of my college years, it became obvious to me that while a lot of corporate recruiters were on campus trying to hire many of my classmates, no one was very interested in a former football player who was rapidly going blind. Understanding that I probably would never get a job, the only logical course of action I could imagine was to start my own business. I told my father about my entrepreneurial aspirations, and he introduced me to the only self-made millionaire that he knew.

Lee Braxton was born early in the 20th century and dropped out of school in the sixth grade during the depths of the Great Depression to start a business to support his family. Due to his amazing drive and talent, Mr. Braxton became a multimillionaire, gave away most of his money to charity, and lived the rest of his life managing his investments.

I met Lee Braxton late in his life, and he became the next great influence in my world.

I discovered Mr. Braxton to be an elderly, gruff, and somewhat abrupt individual at our first encounter. He thrust a book at me entitled *Think and Grow Rich* by Napoleon Hill, saying, "Read this, then come back, and we'll talk."

I had never heard of the book nor the author but began reading and discovered Napoleon Hill, who had been dead for over a decade at that time, to be the next great influence on my career and success.

Napoleon Hill was born in the 19th century and changed the world in the 20th century primarily through the books he wrote. As a young newspaper reporter, Hill was given the assignment to interview Andrew Carnegie, the founder of US Steel and one of the richest men in the world at that time. Napoleon Hill asked Carnegie the secret of becoming rich, and Carnegie's answer influenced Napoleon Hill and the world for generations to come.

Carnegie explained to young Napoleon Hill that no one had ever really quantified the secret to success and wealth, but if Hill would be willing to commit the next 20 years of his life to uncovering these secrets, Andrew Carnegie would open the doors. Napoleon Hill agreed to take up the challenge, and Andrew Carnegie introduced him to hundreds of the most successful and prominent people of the day, including Thomas Edison, Henry Ford, Helen Keller, and many others.

These hundreds of success interviews were synthesized by Napoleon Hill into his book *Think and Grow Rich*, which was released in 1937 and remains the bestselling book of its kind to this day.

After reading *Think and Grow Rich*, I returned to meet with Mr. Braxton, and he made Napoleon Hill's words come to life as he taught me how to be an entrepreneur. Years later when I had achieved my own success and become a multimillionaire myself, I chronicled my journey from poverty to prosperity, including my time with Mr. Braxton and the influence of Napoleon Hill, in a book I entitled *The Millionaire Map*.

Don Green who runs The Napoleon Hill Foundation read my book and called me with a question that astounds me to this day. Don asked, "Jim, did you know that your mentor Mr. Braxton and Napoleon Hill were best friends?" I was in shock, and Don went on to explain that Lee Braxton had given the eulogy at Napoleon Hill's funeral in 1970.

Don Green gave me a file of letters written over a 20-year period between Napoleon Hill and Lee Braxton. I treasure these letters, and they will become the basis for a future book of mine, but until then, they provide me with ongoing reminders of the power of influence.

In the coming chapters, with the able guidance of my coauthor, Dr. Ray Hull, you will begin to understand the influences in your own life and learn how you can make them your slaves instead of your masters.

CHAPTER TWO

COMMUNICATION AS A POWERFUL SOURCE OF INFLUENCE

RAY H. HULL, PhD

INTRODUCTION

This chapter comes in two parts, both detailing the tremendous influence that communication has in any environment, and the critical nature of communication that influences the success of any workplace environment or, in fact, any business venture. Included are (1) the influence of communication and how it can make or break a workplace; (2) the influence of the atmosphere of communication in the workplace; and (3) in some respects, the influence of public relations and image in communication.

THE POWER AND INFLUENCE OF EFFECTIVE COMMUNICATION

Communication is a powerful source of influence. Those who communicate well, with confidence, with speech that is articulate, with the power that interpersonal communication can generate when used effectively and with precision, will be the ones who become the most influential and will succeed in most endeavors. Success in one's professional life depends to a large degree upon their ability to communicate effectively with their clients and colleagues. In other words, to demonstrate excellence as professionals, we must also develop excellence as communicators. The potential influence of an excellent communicator is limitless. This chapter will provide (1) insights into the power of communication and its influence on others in one's professional life and (2) the components of communication that can influence others in business and personal life.

The importance of learning to communicate effectively in our professional life or, I should say, any aspect or endeavor in one's life cannot be overstated. The reason? Much of what professionals in any field do in their daily lives involves communication in one form or another. The better they are, the more influential they will be. For example, we generally choose among health care providers of equal skill and qualifications those who communicate with us most effectively, those who make us feel most comfortable. In fact, that is generally how we select others who serve us—our dentist, our optometrist, our dermatologist, the veterinarian for our four-legged family members, our hair dresser, and even the grocery store where we shop.

However, some professionals are not as effective in the interpersonal aspects of communication as they would desire because they are not skilled in attending to all of the unpredictable events that occur during such interactions, may not be as adept at meeting the needs of those with whom they are communicating, or may not have been prepared. Therefore, they may not be successful in their interactions with those they serve and those with whom they associate as they work to build their business, provide services on behalf of their clients, or interact professionally or personally with their colleagues within their work settings.

Effective communication involves a delicate balance between a nurturing and caring communicative style and the assurance that one is working with a well-prepared professional. But the art of communication with your customers, your clients, and your colleagues can be learned. However, the programs that prepare professionals in the vast majority of fields of service, including medicine, dentistry, cosmetology, carpentry, plumbing, landscaping, and most others, do not offer formal preparation in this critically important aspect of their profession. *This is a sad state for any profession since communication plays a vitally important role in attracting and maintaining one's clientele.*

I COULD NOT COMMUNICATE

For many years of my life, from early childhood through my young adult years, I could not communicate. I was undoubtedly the poorest example of excellence in communication I can imagine. I could not speak without stuttering. Being a severe stutterer, I was not able to say my name, say "hello" on the telephone, ask a young lady out for a date, or speak an entire sentence without embarrassing myself and the person or persons who were listening to me. The majority of the time, I could not utter an entire sentence—period.

I "cured" myself of that awful disorder by placing myself in every situation I could think of that required speaking. I auditioned for every theatrical production throughout high school, college, and beyond; every musical production (since I had a nice singing voice and didn't stutter when I sang); and every public speaking competition I could find to enter.

When I was 16 years old, I even talked the manager of a local radio station into allowing me to start a half-hour, late afternoon, rock-and-roll radio show Monday through Friday of each week. After a short time, it grew to a one-hour, daily show. In front of a microphone with no one watching, I didn't stutter—much. I could produce the banter that came with being a rock-and-roll disk jockey, but little else.

The premise behind all of those speaking efforts was that if I had moments of success in speaking without stuttering, my confidence would grow and the stuttering would become less. At least I hoped that that strategy would work. Success should breed more success, and that was what I was counting on. And it worked! After more than 15 years of successes and failures in acting and public speaking, my times of fluency outnumbered my stuttering failures, and I was speaking fluently, even winning public speaking competitions during the latter years of my college life!

Since then, I have become a sought-after public speaker on the topic of "The Art of Communication" across our nation and the world! I achieved something that I had severe doubts that I would ever achieve. I could talk! And I could motivate others on the topic of "communication" through something I thought I would never be able to achieve—public speaking—and I have the rare opportunity to influence others with my words of advice, instruction, and encouragement and to challenge my audiences to communicate with authority, direction, and enthusiasm!

HOW DO WE INFLUENCE OTHERS THROUGH COMMUNICATION?

One of the comments I hear all too frequently as I advise others about effective communication is, "I tell my employees what we need to do to increase our sales capacity, but then later I notice that most of them are headed in the wrong direction—again!" I may respond to her or him by saying, "Well, it may be that they didn't understand what you said." The look I receive from the person is generally a look of astonishment, apparently thinking, "I was perfectly clear. They probably just weren't listening!" It is obvious that the bosses from whom I hear that comment have not become acquainted with the tasks involved in effective communication, the kind of communication that influences others to move in the direction they hoped would occur.

When I am working with those who find themselves in leadership positions within business and industry, I stress to them that clear and effective communication is not only essential to good leadership but is also an essential ingredient within leadership that *influences* others in positive ways, that *motivates* them to move in the direction that the leader intended. In other words, the recipients of the advice understood what was said, were *motivated*, and in turn, began to move in the direction that the leader had intended in the first place.

In other words, the leader is then discovering probably the most important ingredient in both effective leadership and the ability to be a positive influence in the lives of their employees. By using clear and effective communication, they find that the employees hear and, most importantly, understand the direction or the request that was given to them. That doesn't seem to be a difficult task, but it all too frequently seems to be the catalyst for leaders' frustration in business, industry, education, and other work environments. They think that they communicated clearly, but they apparently did not.

Chen feels that there is a need to explore the relationship between communication within complex organizations and the performance of workers since communication is the integrating component between organizational units and the functions within an organization. He feels that communication is the activity that links people and creates relationships within organizations. For instance, he says that communication is the "glue" that binds people together within an organization.[1] And managers are the key to good communication within any working environment. Effective communication improves job performance among workers, while poor communication can result in low employee commitment to the work environment.[2]

Let's look at the three factors that impact effectiveness in communication in the workplace or, for that matter, any communicative environment.

THE INFLUENCE OF COMMUNICATION AND HOW COMMUNICATION CAN MAKE OR BREAK THE WORKPLACE

Since the 1990s, companies have become dependent on email as their primary connection with clients and colleagues.

Even employees sitting one cubicle apart are emailing rather than talking to one another! But we need to remember that *effective* communication is critical to your success.

Here are some suggestions on how we can improve communication in any work environment.

THE POSITIVE INFLUENCE OF FACE-TO-FACE COMMUNICATION

Communication specialists have observed that we have become so dependent on our computers and iPhones that we have neglected, or perhaps even lost, the art of conversation—of actually talking to one another. The problem is that up to 70% of the meaning of what we say to one another comes not from the words that we use but from our facial expressions and our body language. If we take smiles and gestures out of the picture by interacting only via computer, the recipient of our messages may get the wrong idea regarding our intent, especially if the sender is not a particularly articulate writer. The way to overcome this is to pick up the phone and make a call once in a while or walk down the hallway to talk to our colleagues or employees face-to-face.

THE INFLUENCE OF GOOD LISTENING SKILLS

A common barrier to communication in the workplace is the negative influence of poor listening skills. What causes that to happen? We may be distracted with concerns over other matters. We may be listening but appear not to be because we're not directly attending to the person who is talking to us. We may be concerned about time and attend to our watch or the clock on the wall rather than the person who is expressing a concern. There are many reasons why we may not be a good listener.

To correct that, we must not only listen to the person who is speaking to us by concentrating on her or his face and intentionally attending to what is being said but also by reflecting on what the person is saying.

Good listeners do the following: They give the speaker (the one to whom they are listening) cues that they are listening. That means being empathetic and responsive to what the person is saying:

- They maintain good eye contact and *no* side glances. That's a dead giveaway that they are not really interested in what the person is saying. They also do not look at their watch!

- They show the person who is sharing their thoughts that they are listening carefully to what is being said.

- They offer verbal expressions of feeling: for example, "That must have made you very angry."

A PROBLEM OF PERCEPTION

There has been one constant in workplace communication. That constant has been and continues to be that of "perception." The primary problem with perception is that we all look at the world differently. In order to not allow perception to be a barrier to communication in the workplace, remember that there are always many viewpoints and opinions among those persons with whom we work. And, in listening to those varied viewpoints and opinions, new ideas and approaches to problem solving may arise.

THE PROBLEM OF MICROMANAGERS

Everyone has had at least one micromanager in their career. This person is like a shadow, lurking in the background, making sure everyone is doing their job. They appear to feel as though they hired incompetents. Hopefully however, personnel were hired with the skills and intelligence to do their job well. So, there is no reason to hover over them. Further, by doing so, they stifle communication. Employees do not enjoy communicating with them, so they try very hard not to.

When employees feel as though they have control of their responsibilities, they tend to feel a sense of purpose and are more invested in the process of doing an excellent job. Further, they will tend to communicate openly with their manager. If we provide employees the tools they need to get their job done and then give them the freedom to do it, they will. Managers need to remember that if they desire their most productive workforce!

THE ATMOSPHERE OF COMMUNICATION

Here is another aspect of communication that is critical to your success in any work environment. That involves the *atmosphere* of communication.

Much of what we do in our day-to-day interactions with employees and others involves communication in one form or another. But, interpersonal communication goes beyond talking.

Much beyond simply talking, interpersonal communication includes the creation of an "atmosphere" of communication that results in a positive and constructive work environment. It creates a positive environment for productivity and creativity. And the better we are at creating that environment, the more successful we and our organization will become.

We are drawn to those who make us feel most comfortable, who communicate with us in a positive and supportive manner. It is, in the end, what separates a successful organizational environment from those that are less successful.

So, what does it involve?

Interpersonal communication in a work environment not only involves what we *say*, but very importantly, what we *do* in our communicative interactions with others. What we *do* may involve our body language, the gestures that we use, our manner of eye contact, and *very* importantly, the manner in which we listen. Remember, good listeners become good leaders.

I tell my audiences, "Whether we want to or not, we live in a world of people who do not communicate well. But we also live in a world of people who do not possess the knowledge or skill to be good communicators. It is simply that many people, including many bosses, may possess communication habits that are less than desirable."

THE REASONS?

1. **They use poor body language**—Hands in pockets, shuffling feet, shoulders hunched forward, poor eye contact are all indicators that the listener is really not interested in what is being said.

2. **They may use inappropriate grooming**—Extreme clothing or makeup, clothing that is designed for evening party wear, extreme hairstyles, visible body piercings, and extreme tattoos distract from positive interactive communication.

3. **They interrupt the conversation**—Interrupting by interjecting their opinion before their associate has finished speaking shuts down communication.

4. **They do not return messages**—Telephone or email messages that are not responded to in a reasonable amount of time reveal an attitude of not caring.

These and many more causes of poor communication in a work environment can result in employees who will cease communicating with those who are responsible for them. The positive influence of effective communication is what keeps a business, a hospital, or a clinic functioning creatively and successfully.

THE INFLUENCE OF PUBLIC RELATIONS AND IMAGE

Here is another very influential component of successful communication in the workplace, but from a slightly different angle. This involves the art of public relations and image that enhances the success of any work environment.

One's ability to impress their customers, their clients, makes or breaks a business whether it be a commercial enterprise, a dental practice, or a church where the minister is the center of focus. Here, I am referring to one's ability to demonstrate the quality of what they do every day and the sincerity of effort that drives what they do. If the services that are being provided are of the highest quality, and the knowledge and skill that is necessary to assure the public that they are capable of maintaining that quality is consistently demonstrated, then the enterprise *should* do well. Right?

I have emphasized the word *should* in the sentence above. The reason? The reason is that there are many in businesses and medical and non-medical practices, including hairdressers, plumbers, electricians, salespeople, and so on, who possess the knowledge and skill to be a success but do not achieve the level that they should because of the image that they portray and/or their ability to demonstrate a positive public image that would allow them to achieve a high level of success.

How do we achieve the level of success that one dreams of? Here it is—The processes involved in enhancing our professional image and the art of public relations involves *communication* at one of the highest levels!

Here are some suggestions that will assist not only in building a good professional image but also in building excellent public relations for one's business or practice:

THE ART AND INFLUENCE OF IMAGE BUILDING

- No matter how bad the day, don't place it on your clients or associates by telling them about it!

- Be appropriate in all behaviors—no off-color jokes or remarks, no matter how innocent they appear to you.

- Be pleasant, be a genuinely good person, be empathetic, be nice!

- Be a good ambassador of your profession.

- If a client comes to you wanting their money returned or is making some other demand, no matter what the reason, think, "If I were the client or the customer, how would I want this handled"?

- "How would I respond if that person was my relative or my friend?" Then, handle it that way.

- Always remember this rule—We are here to serve, not to judge.

- Work hard to be a flexible and creative problem solver.

- Affirm your commitment to serving people and your enthusiasm about the opportunity!

- Listen carefully and quietly to what the other person is saying, no matter how urgently you want them to know that you already have the solution to their problem. Don't interrupt!

- When listening, NEVER look at your watch!

- Be empathetic, but never respond by saying, "I know just how you feel," unless you have clearly experienced what the other person is expressing.

- Remember to speak at a slightly slower rate than your usual speed of speech. You will be much more easily understood.

- When you slow your rate of speech, a natural result is that you will articulate with greater clarity.

- Maintain good eye contact, but do not stare at the person you are speaking with. For best eye contact, concentrate on the other person's nose. Do NOT look into their eyes. That level of intimacy is not appropriate unless you intend to ask the person to marry you!

- Remember what Sam Walton taught us: "There is only one boss—the customer."

- Sam Walton's three rules for success in business:
  - Rule No. 1: The customer is always right.
  - Rule No. 2: The customer is always right.
  - Rule No. 3: The customer is always right.

INFLUENCING OTHERS THROUGH EFFECTIVE COMMUNICATION

I was approached by a business manager who was frustrated because he felt that he had good ideas on how to move the business forward in positive ways but had a difficult time motivating his employees. He noticed that although his employees seem to understand his ideas and the motives behind them, he found that they simply continude on the same path without making the changes he was recommending.

Rosabeth Moss Kanter of the Harvard School of Business states that "Getting ideas off the ground requires personal credibility and positive power." To achieve that, she gives *Four Influencing Strategies:*[3]

1. **Showing Up: The Power of Presence.** She says that it is a truth that 90% of success in life comes from simply showing up! She stresses the power of face-to-face communication with those you serve as opposed to continual

communication via digital means. Walking down the hallway to speak to a colleague carries much more meaning than sending an email message.

2. **Speaking Up: The Power of Voice.** Kanter says that speaking up carries a great deal of weight in getting your ideas across to others. Putting your ideas into words and presenting them in an articulate manner is what causes people to listen to you and perhaps see you as their leader. She recommends that if you are not comfortable with speaking in public, find a coach and take lessons. Toastmaster and Toastmistress Clubs are wonderful ways to become more comfortable speaking in public and to speak with greater confidence and skill.

3. **Teaming Up: The Power of Partnering.** Kanter also recommends that if you move into leadership roles, your singular knowledge and skills are probably not enough. Building good relationships with others who can assist you—who will partner with you—will help you develop ideas and avenues for program/business advancements. Two minds are frequently better than just one in developing ideas and programs. But remember that two is better than three. In a triad, one of the three will generally attempt to become the leader, and it may not be you!

THE POWER OF PERSISTENCE

Not giving up can become a powerful motto for any leader in any endeavor. Sometimes you may feel like giving up. But giving up doesn't get things done. Those who eventually succeed just keep on going—they don't give up. If you have a good idea that you are very sure will work, you may have some self-doubts along the way—"Was it really a good idea? Maybe it wasn't, but I still think that it will work!" Successful people have self-doubts, but they don't give up. They keep moving forward until they succeed.

HOW DOES COMMUNICATION INFLUENCE OTHERS?

How do I know if I am communicating well? That is a question I am asked quite frequently. Here is my response. Effective interpersonal communication does not mean always communicating perfectly. I have never met anyone who communicates perfectly. Rather, it means being able to constructively create and convey appropriate responses to those with whom we are communicating and to perhaps identify and explain creative solutions that are acceptable to them. It means motivating others to positive change through direct verbal interaction, nonverbal interaction (what we don't say), our body language, and a *positive* atmosphere of communication.

I like the phrase "positive atmosphere of communication." The reason I like it is because it provides a framework for communication that is constructive and successful. Rather than communicating perfectly, I like to think in terms of communicating *constructively*—or *meaningfully*. When we communicate constructively, we are more apt to be communicating in a meaningful way.

SO, IN THE END, WHAT IS IT?

Recently I read a well-written treatise on communication found on UK Web Archive. It said, in part, "interpersonal communication is the process by which people exchange information and feelings through verbal and nonverbal messages."[4] That is a very straightforward definition.

The authors continue, "Interpersonal communication is not only about what is actually said—the words and language used—but *how* it is said, and the nonverbal messages sent through tone of voice, facial expressions, gestures and body language." Again, very straightforward!

The authors explain that when two or more people are in the same place and are aware of each other's presence, one way or another, communication is taking place, no matter how subtle or unintentional or how poorly it is being handled.

IS SPEECH NECESSARY?

Using speech is not necessary. Without speech, an observer may be observing the cues of posture, facial expression, and dress to form an impression of the other's role, emotional state, personality and/or intentions. Although no communication may be intended, people receive messages through forms of nonverbal behavior.

SOME PRINCIPLES OF INTERPERSONAL COMMUNICATION

The authors continue by giving principles of interpersonal communication that I personally like. They govern the effectiveness of communication. However, as the authors say, even though these principles are generally quite simple, they will often take a lifetime to master. They are presented as follows:

Interpersonal Communication Is Not Optional

We may, at times, try not to communicate; but *not* communicating is not an option. In fact, the harder we try not to communicate, the more we are communicating! By not communicating, we are communicating *something*, perhaps that we are shy, perhaps that we are angry or sulking, perhaps that we are too busy to talk. Ignoring somebody is communicating with them. We may not tell them we are ignoring them, but through our nonverbal means of communication we make that apparent.

Again, nonverbal communication can be just as and, many times, more powerful than the words that we use. Our body posture and position and our eye contact (or lack of it) are all important. Even the smallest and most subtle of mannerisms communicate something to others.

Communication Is Irreversible

Interpersonal communication is irreversible. Perhaps we can wish we had not said something. We feel a sense of regret and apologize for something we said, but we can't take it back. We often behave toward and therefore communicate with others based on previous communication encounters. But those encounters may or may not be appropriate points of reference. Because of these stereotypes, when we communicate with people, we may carry with us certain preconceptions of what the other person is thinking or how they are likely to behave. We may also have ideas about the outcome of the conversation before it even begins as a result of our pre-knowledge of the person or the circumstances in which the conversation is taking place.

We need to start all interpersonal communication with an open mind; listen to what is being said rather than hearing what we *expect* to hear. As a result, we are less likely to be misunderstood or say things that we later regret.

The Context of Communication

Communication happens for a reason. To help avoid misunderstandings and therefore communicate more effectively, it is important that the context of the communication is understood by all. Why is the communication happening? It is important that participants are on the same "wavelength" so that they understand why the communication is occurring. We may think that "why" is clearly evident, but it may not be clear to all who are involved. It must be clearly understood why the communication event is taking place. The best question to ask everyone may be, "Do you understand why we are getting together at this time?" Misunderstandings can be avoided with that simple question.

IN CONCLUSION

As I stated at the beginning of this chapter, communication is a powerful source of influence. Those who communicate well, with confidence, with speech that is articulate, with the power that interpersonal communication can generate when used effectively and with precision, will be the ones who become the most influential and will succeed in most endeavors. Success in one's professional life depends to a large degree upon their ability to communicate effectively with their clients and colleagues. In other words, to demonstrate excellence as professionals, we must also develop excellence as communicators.

Influence begins with communication. It doesn't begin with our size, our heritage, or our looks. It begins with how we communicate, how we influence others with our words, and how we present ourselves, our poise, and our demeanor.

CHAPTER THREE

TWO-WAY INFLUENCE

*Every day, in every way, we are influenced
by others just as we influence them.*
—JIM STOVALL

Just as we can manifest any influence in our lives as either a positive or negative force, every encounter we have can influence both us and everyone involved.

There are countless numbers of people to whom I owe my success. As an interviewer—both for books and columns as well as on television—I have had the privilege of meeting and interviewing some of the greatest people of the 20th and now the 21st century. These people represent the top achievers from the arenas of politics, movies, sports, and television. Many of these superstars have had a lasting influence on my life.

During publicity tours for our work on television as well as my new books and movies, I am often asked by reporters which person has impacted my life the most. I have thought a lot about it, and there is one special individual who has had a lasting influence on me.

Shortly after I learned of my impending blindness, I decided to continue with my plans to attend a local university. Near the university, there is a school for blind children, and I'm not sure if my motives were to learn more about blindness, make some kind of bargain with God, or just to help out; but in any event, I went to the school for blind children and met the principal.

I told her that I was a college freshman, and I had no background, training, or experience working with blind children, and I would like to teach in her school. You can imagine how excited she was to see me! But she was a kind soul and told me that if I really wanted to, they had one child I could work with one-on-one.

I agreed, and she explained that Christopher was four years old, was totally blind, and had many other physical problems. Following their many tests, they had determined that Christopher would never develop or advance any more than he already had. And what they wanted me to do was keep him quiet and keep him away from the other kids so they could learn their lessons.

As I look back on it today, I realize that Christopher was suffering from the most severe disability of all—that is, being faced with no expectations. We always live up to the expectations that we have of ourselves or those expectations that we allow other people to place upon us.

They had no expectations for Christopher, and the only training they gave me were two very simple things. First, they instructed me to keep his shoes tied, as they were afraid he would trip and fall because he had never learned to tie his shoelaces. Secondly, they told me I had to keep him away from the stairs because he had never learned to climb the stairs, and they were afraid he would fall down the staircase.

Other than those two things, they really didn't care what I did as long as I kept Christopher quiet so that the other students could learn their lessons.

That first day, I was introduced to Christopher and immediately noticed that he was much smaller than you would expect a four-year-old child to be, and he was, indeed, totally blind and had many other physical problems.

He and I sat down and had a serious conversation, and I told him, "Young man, before I leave here, no matter how many weeks or months or even years it takes, you are at least going to learn how to tie your shoes and climb the stairs."

And he replied, "No, I can't."

And I responded, "Yes, you can."

And he replied, "No, I can't."

And I responded, "Yes, you can."

And he replied, "No, I can't . . ."

If you have ever spent any length of time with a four-year-old child, you know that they can argue like this all day long.

Christopher and I began working every day, learning how to tie his shoes and climb the stairs. Meanwhile, I was attending the university and facing what I thought were insurmountable obstacles. I couldn't see well enough to get around anymore and couldn't read the textbooks.

When it got difficult, I simply prepared to quit once again.

I went to the school for blind children for what I thought would be my last day. I met with the principal and told her that because of my own visual impairment, I was going to drop out of college, so I wouldn't be able to come here and work with Christopher anymore because I simply couldn't make it.

I didn't realize that Christopher had been dropped off early that morning, and he was standing outside the open door to the office, hearing our entire conversation. So, as I went out to tell him goodbye and tell him that I loved him and tell him that I hoped that someday someone else would show up and spend some time with him, he turned to me and repeated my own words back at me by saying, "Yes, you can!"

And I replied, "No, I can't."

And he persisted, "Yes, you can!"

And as I replied, "No, I can't" once again, I was mentally preparing an explanation so I could justify to Christopher how my challenges were somehow different or greater than his were. But, before I could begin my weak explanation, it hit me like a ton of bricks. The obvious answer was, "Stovall, either get up and do something with your life, or quit lying to this poor kid in telling him he can do things in his life."

Three years later, I graduated from that university with honors. And the same week, I had the privilege of my life, with what little vision I had left, to observe then-seven-year-old Christopher climb three flights of stairs, turn and sit on the top step, and tie both of his shoes.

About six weeks after the miraculous day when Christopher climbed the stairs and tied his shoes, he died of a brain tumor. The tumor was the condition that had caused him to lose his sight in the first place, and eventually it took his life.

As I was attending his funeral, one of the other teachers said to me, "Isn't it a shame we'll never know how much he could have developed or contributed had he been given a full life?"

I told her that he had already made his contribution because anything I did from that point forward, I would owe to him.

They tell me that I have shared Christopher's story with over a million people, live in events around the world, and now I am sharing it with you through this book. Many of those people—and hopefully you—will be influenced by Christopher's example as a platform to examine your dreams, take possession of them, remove the obstacles, eliminate the excuses, and realize that any dream you have inside of you is well within your capacity to achieve.

When Christopher died, it was almost as if he had a will. He left me three separate things that I want to pass on to you.

First, Christopher left me with the certain knowledge that there is no such thing as an insignificant person. If God had ever created an insignificant person, it would have been Christopher. His whole biography would read, "Christopher lived to be seven years old. He learned how to tie his shoes and climb the stairs." These were all of the accomplishments that Christopher could claim after his brief life, but he influenced the lives of thousands of people around the world through his example of courage.

Secondly, Christopher left me with the certain knowledge that there is no such thing as an insignificant relationship. All relationships are critical. Each of them is important. There are people in your world who are struggling. They're trying to decide whether their dreams can come true. They will be greatly influenced by what you say and, more importantly, what you do with your own struggles in your own life.

And finally, Christopher left me with the certain knowledge that there is no such thing as an insignificant day because when you live your life in the present, every day of the rest of your life holds within it your key to greatness, which is your ability to build on your past and create your future by living out your destiny today.

My intentions and efforts to influence Christopher were dwarfed by the influence he had and continues to have on me and, consequently, millions of other people around the world.

In my academic field of psychology, probably the most practical discovery of the last generation is the fact that we become like the five people with whom we spend the most time. Once we realize we will assume the mannerisms, speech, opinions, and even the income of the five people we hang around with most, we should all be challenged to be more selective with respect to whom we allow to influence us.

My mentor and the publisher of my first novel, Charlie "Tremendous" Jones, was fond of saying, "You will be the same person you are today five years from now except for the people you meet and the books you read." Charlie was one of the greatest proponents of literacy and reading. He also realized that we can be influenced not only by the people we interact with daily but any historical figure we choose to read about.

If you don't have five role models in your current sphere of influence that you would like to emulate, you must realize that Benjamin Franklin, Leonardo da Vinci, Helen Keller, Thomas Edison, and countless others are just waiting to become positive influences upon your future within the pages of a book.

If we are going to seek out people to influence us, it is critical that we select the right individuals. I'm a firm believer in the principle that we should never take advice from anyone who doesn't have what we want. Broke financial planners, overweight diet gurus, and imprisoned lawyers should be avoided at all costs.

Our grandparents were greatly influenced by people with whom they interacted on a daily basis. We have that same element of influence but have the added input from the media. The internet has opened up a world of information to us, but like most things it can be either a positive or negative influence.

We are bombarded constantly with media messages designed to get our attention and influence us with products, services, and advice. Much of this influence is ineffective or dysfunctional, and some of it is actually dangerous. If you're going to spend your time and risk your future on someone else's influence in your life, make sure they have what you want and are not just someone trying to sell you something or take advantage of you.

Everybody wants to climb the mountain of success, but only a few people have been to the summit. If you're going to take someone's advice and be influenced by them, it's much better to select someone who is coming down from the mountaintop than someone who is climbing on the same trail you are currently on.

Once you find high-quality influencers in your life, it's good to dig deeper and find out what influences them. Influential people can introduce you to other successful individuals and recommend great books, movies, videos, and experiences that have made a difference in their lives.

Influence should never be a one-way street. Napoleon Hill introduced the world to the mastermind concept, which is simply a group of like-minded individuals committed to one another's success who are willing to share their influence with the group and reap the rewards of how the group can influence them.

Just as in my relationship with Christopher, often you will set out to influence someone else by making a difference in their life and find that you are the one that receives the greatest rewards.

Here in the 21st century, there are countless media outlets and internet sources seeking our time and attention. You must control this onslaught of images and not let it control you. The influence of the media is subtle and immensely powerful.

I am in the television industry through my company the Narrative Television Network which makes movies, TV, and educational programming accessible to the 13 million blind and visually impaired Americans as well as millions more around the world. In the television industry, they promote what I call The Big Lie which demonstrates the powerful influence of the media. The Big Lie tells us that the average high school graduate who has seen thousands of murders, acts of violence, and reprehensible behavior on television is not influenced by these images because they know it's make-believe; but if a corporation will spend millions of dollars for a 30-second commercial, the sales of their products will skyrocket due to the influence of the commercial. It's obvious that regardless of what Big Lies the industry may tell, the programming as well as the advertising we watch influences us and changes our behavior.

An even more insidious influence on young people today are the countless videogames that create an alternative universe in which the participants can perform violent acts or be involved in other damaging distractions under the guise of playing a game.

Everything we do, everything we watch, and everything we confront influences us and how we perform. If you are going to succeed, you've got to control and even plan the TV and movies you watch, the games you play, and the part of the internet you allow to influence you. Social media not only influences how we think and act, but it can impact how we influence others for years to come.

Our parents and grandparents all made mistakes and did things they wish they hadn't done, but they didn't immortalize it like so many people do today via social media. Just remember, images from the party you attended or the practical joke you played on someone posted to the internet will be a permanent influence on your future and what people will think of you.

In the past, it may have been enough to know that our minds are influenced by outside forces, but today, we must be mindful of the fact that these outside sources can influence what people think of us and how we may succeed or fail in the future.

We are always being influenced and influencing others. We must act wisely if we are to reach our goals and live the lives of our dreams.

CHAPTER FOUR

THE POWER AND
INFLUENCE OF IMAGE
AND PUBLIC RELATIONS

RAY H. HULL, PhD

have over 25 years of experience coaching professionals in the art of professional image, interpersonal communication, and public relations, and more than 30 years of experience in coaching professionals in the art of public speaking. Further, I have published numerous articles on the topic of communication and the influence of image, interpersonal communication, and the power of nonverbal communication in our professional lives.

Our ability to impress our clients with our professionalism, our support, our skill as specialists in our fields and our ability to provide a competent, nurturing, caring service on behalf of our clients makes or breaks our professional reputation in any service environment. I am referring to our ability to demonstrate the quality of what we do every day and the sincerity of effort that drives what we do in the long term. If the services that we are providing are of the highest quality, then we *should* do well. Right?

I have emphasized the word *should* in the sentence above. The reason? The reason is that there are many professional businesses with personnel who possess the knowledge and skill to be successful but do not succeed because of the image they portray and/or their ability to demonstrate a positive public image and the level of public relations that would allow them to achieve a high level of success. And we must remember that public relations in our professional lives involve who we are, the image that we portray, and how we impress those who make decisions about who they will do business with!

How do we achieve the level of success that we dream of? The processes involved in enhancing our *professional image and the art of public relations* involves *communication* at one of its highest levels. That is because the image that we portray to those with whom we associate on a daily basis, including our boss, our colleagues, and importantly, our clients, makes or breaks our career.

Image involves the way we dress, speak, the way we interact with others, even our posture, and our manner of presenting ourselves to others. We need to ask ourselves, "Am I the kind of person my boss and colleagues want to work with and our customers want to be served by?" In the end, that means being *authentic, positive, and polite*. It means creating the *personal charm* that persuades and makes others feel at ease. You then become the person with whom others desire to associate and by whom clients feel comfortable being served.

The following list gives some suggestions that will not only assist in building a good professional image and enhance the level of public image/public relations we want to develop, but also assist in building excellent public visibility for one's business or practice Some of them are also found in Chapter 2, but are thought to also be appropriate here:

THE ART OF IMAGE:

- Don't tell your customers or associates how bad your day has been. They probably do not want to hear about it!

- Do your best to be pleasant, to be a genuinely good person, to be empathetic, to be nice! You will become much more attractive to your customers and your associates.

- I was told many times by my professors during my doctoral preparation that in order to be successful, it was imperative to be a good ambassador for my profession, and create a positive atmosphere wherever my services are provided.

- Always remember this rule—we are here to serve, not to judge.

- Affirm your commitment to serving people and your enthusiasm for the opportunity!

- Listen carefully and quietly to what the other person is saying no matter how urgently we want them to know that we already have the solution to their problem!

- When listening, NEVER look at your watch!

- Public perception of you determines to a sizeable degree how successful you and your organization or business will be.

- If your patients are receiving thorough and competent services, and your behavior toward them is nurturing, caring, thoughtful, and trustworthy, then they will "sing your praises" to others in your community, and your business or organization will grow.

- We must affirm our commitment to serving people and our enthusiasm for it.

THE INFLUENCE OF PROFESSIONAL IMAGE AND PUBLIC RELATIONS

I was reading a treatise on the influence of professional image recently entitled "Professional Image," in which Yasmin Anderson-Smith, President of KYMS Image International, said, "It may seem somewhat unfair to judge an individual by appearance and behavior rather than exclusively on performance, but in most business environments, judgments are made about people based on the professional image they display as a result of appearance and behavior. This occurs before the individual's level of competence or performance is determined."

Therefore, it has been found that the impact of professional image can be substantial, particularly in the business world.[5]

Anderson-Smith continues by giving advice to those who strive to improve their professional image.[6]

Those include:

1. Dress to impress. Your image matters. In other words, dress the way you want to be addressed in your occupational life.

2. Make sure that your social skills are up to par. Errors in social environments will not only embarrass you but also quickly lower your personal image.

3. Build your own "personal brand" that will allow you to stand out with distinction in a positive way.

4. Grow a network of colleagues that can also be friends and supporters.

5. Be likeable. Adopt a positive attitude. In other words, be positive in your daily life at work and at play.

6. Watch what you write. There is a vast difference between the cryptic language and spelling used on the iPhone and the spelling and language used when communicating via email or letter. Perfect your writing skills (spelling, grammar, punctuation) to impress those with whom you are communicating electronically or by mail.

7. Look at yourself in the mirror. What do you see? Shirts and pants that need ironing? Dresses that are too short? A tie hanging at an angle on a shirt that is the wrong color?

Tattoos showing on arms or neck? Blue jeans rather than professional slacks? A blouse that is a little too revealing? Make sure that what you see is how you want your boss to know you.

That list can go on and on. In the end, what you see in that professional mirror should be what we would expect of a professional in your field of work. If the image you see isn't what you would imagine it should be, consult an advisor from a men's or women's clothing store—one who you trust—or confide in your boss or her/his assistant and ask them to give you a direct appraisal of your appearance or manner of dress—not an appraisal to make you feel better about yourself but a truly direct, brutal appraisal. Your boss or her/his assistant will probably be flattered that you confided in them.

WHAT IS PROFESSIONAL IMAGE? HOW IS IT DEVELOPED?

According to "What is a Professional Image?" from the American Association of Employment in Education, professional image involves a set of qualities and characteristics that represent perceptions of your competence and character by your clients and your peers.[7]

Image is your representation of you, "the message" of who you are and what you represent. Image involves a lasting first impression.

Remember, you only have one chance to make a first impression. That includes the *two minute rule*. A lasting first impression involves the image that you portray during the first two minutes of entering a room for an interview or discussion. Those who may have never seen or met you before make their decision based on their impression of you within the first two minutes. That impression is made even as you first enter the room. And that first impression and the decision about you is difficult to erase.

You must avoid negativity. A negative person is no fun to be around. The doom and gloom that they carry with them can destroy the potential for positive relationships with their colleagues and their boss. People like people who see the good in their work environment and the good in others, who are happy to see their colleagues and clients when they arrive in the morning, who don't carry the bad news they heard on television or radio that morning with them when they talk with their colleagues or clients. People like people who are happy, or at least act happy during the day.

Don't say bad or negative things about your past place of employment, your colleagues, or your boss. Those words can take on a life of their own and haunt you. Avoid questionable behaviors or questionable forms of communication. Be the best, most likeable person who can be. Be a good person—the kind of person you would like to be around each day, the kind of person who you would grow to like and admire!

BE A COMMUNICATOR WITH POISE—
USE STRESS TO IMPRESS!

Talking about developing your image and the art of public relations in your professional life, I received a phone call about a week ago from a young woman who wanted to ask me about the process of communication. However, at that moment, she didn't seem to be too sure what she actually wanted to ask. She said during our conversation that she has a difficult time maintaining her composure or her poise during staff meetings. She said that when something she has said in a staff meeting is challenged by a colleague, she tries very hard to remain calm and respond in a professional manner. However, she sometimes "loses it" during their discussion, raises her voice, and uses words that she is embarrassed about later. She said that it distresses her that during staff meetings some of her colleagues are somehow able to goad her into becoming so stressed that she loses her poise and falls apart in front of everyone. She was definitely not impressing her colleagues and customers by her professional image and was not doing well in the arena of public relations!

As we talked, a statement by authors Brett and Kate McKay came to mind, so I shared it with her. It is, "Calmness is the rarest quality in human life."[8] She said that made her feel a little better. But she wanted some specifics on how to maintain her poise in stressful situations. So, I shared with her something that Sherrie Campbell, Clinical Psychologist and expert on mastering poise, has said. It is as follows: "Whenever you are in any working group, or a position of responsibility, one way to remain composed is to remember that you always have an audience. Your team members and other colleagues are your audience, and they expect a certain level of calm, serenity, integrity and grit from you."[9] We can literally be an example of calm and poise! One way is to *think* of yourself as being an example of what your colleagues would like to become when faced with stress.

Here are a few suggestions that I shared with her:

- Let others know how you feel, but do it calmly and perhaps not too vividly!

- In a meeting, never, NEVER take a cheap shot, no matter how good it might make you feel at the moment. You will only regret it later.

- In meetings or in other interpersonal interactions, don't make a big deal out of a trivial issue. If you do, ask yourself "Why?"

- If someone treats you in an unkind manner, practice forgiving, forgetting, and getting over it.

- And, if you see an argument on the horizon, become a good listener instead. Let the other person vent while you listen quietly. You will win many an "argument" that way, and you won't find yourself in the middle of a potentially embarrassing situation.

- In other words, when one person says something that might provoke a negative response or an argument, it is best for us to simply listen quietly no matter how much we would like to enter the fray!

- Remember—you can never truly win an argument.

- The best way to win an argument is to avoid it. Don't participate in it, no matter how sure you are that your opinion is correct and even if you see a golden opportunity to "jump in."

- And, remember—you will never get into trouble by admitting that you may be wrong.

- During a meeting discussion, if we find that what the other person is saying is correct and what we are advocating is probably wrong, even though we sometimes don't want to admit it, there's nothing wrong with looking beyond our ego and admitting, "You know, in thinking about it, I believe that you are right!" That simple response tends to stop a potential argument or an embarrassing situation in its tracks and makes everyone feel better, including you.

Those were the suggestions that I not only gave her, but sent to her as well. I hope they helped. They have helped me!

HOW DO WE DEVELOP OUR OWN "BRAND"?

How do we develop an image that will give us our own "brand" in our professional lives, in our business lives, that will help us to reach the level of positive public relations that we are striving for? If we are going to advance in our career to the highest level, it is imperative that we develop the ability to influence others in positive ways, including our customers, our clients, our superiors, and our colleagues, by the image that we have developed—our professional, public image.

I received an email from one of our former graduates the other day who was frustrated because she did not receive the promotion that she was sure she was going to be offered. One of her colleagues received it instead. She was a person who had graduated at the same time as our graduate and seemed to have the same skill and knowledge level. So, she was wondering what she could have done to convince her employer that she was the most deserving of that promotion at the hospital where she works.

I told our graduate about something that Rosabeth Moss Kanter from the Harvard School of Business has written, as I also cited in Chapter 2 of this book. Kanter gives the following four pieces of advice that may have helped our graduate:[10]

1. **The Power of Presence**. She says that 90% of success in life comes from just showing up! Digital and other remote forms of communication can be efficient, but there's much to be said for being there face-to-face with others during meetings or staff and superiors during other discussions.

2. **Speaking up—The Power of Voice**. This means more than just talking. It means being articulate, putting your spoken ideas into

words in an effective manner. She advises that if you are uncomfortable with speaking in public or at meetings, get a coach, take lessons, or join Toastmasters or Toastmistresses.

3. **The Power of Partnering**. Success depends to a significant degree on building good relationships inside and outside of your place of employment. We must learn to "play well with others" in order to succeed.

4. **The Power of Persistence**. If you tried, and what you were proposing wasn't accepted or the position for which you applied was not offered to you, keep at it, make adjustments, and surprise the naysayers. All successful people deal with self-doubt or rejection—was I good enough, did I say the right thing, am I designed for advancement? Successful people keep going—persistence pays off in the end.

OTHER SUGGESTIONS ON INFLUENCING OTHERS IN POSITIVE WAYS

Here are some other suggestions on how to influence others in positive ways that can help you advance in their professional life by creating a personal image and positive public relations:

1. Confident people tend to be leaders, more so than those who lack a sense of confidence, who, in turn, present themselves in an insecure

manner. Put on a face full of confidence. If you don't feel confident, act confident! By acting confident, you might very well become confident to a greater degree!

2. Know the person you are desiring to influence. As Dale Carnegie has said in his award winning book, *How to Win Friends and Influence People*, "Talk to someone about themselves, and they'll listen for hours. Talk about yourself, and they will stop listening."[11] People will start liking you if you show interest in them first. Get to know them. Make yourself likeable. You will gain their trust.

3. Ensure honesty by being genuine. Be absolutely genuine when working with others. Gaining trust and respect will go a long way toward leading you into higher realms of leadership in your place of employment.

And, as Dale Carnegie states further in his best-selling book, *How to Win Friends and Influence People*, "There are four ways, and only four ways in which we are evaluated by the world (and by our superiors and others we desire to influence). We are evaluated and classified by: What we do, How we look, What we say, and how we say it."[12] If we want to influence others in positive ways, those four are important to live by.

In the two-room rural school I attended that was located in our farming community in central Kansas, we graduated at the conclusion of the eighth grade. Some of us progressed on to high school and college. The children who were from the conservative Mennonite families in that community did not progress onto high school, but rather terminated their formal education at that point. Graduation day was a solemn day for them since they were leaving their friends, the school they had attended for eight years, and the teachers who had taught them—one teacher for grades one through four, and one for grades five through eight. Since for many of the children their formal education would terminate at the end of the eighth grade, we were all taught a number of things that children in regular schools were not—correct table manners, polite behavior in social settings, tolerance of the social and political leanings of others, and many other aspects of life that would be beneficial to us. We were also instructed on how to develop a positive self-image and how to engage in positive public relations that would continue on into our lives. Although our teacher didn't refer directly to the term "public relations," she instructed us on developing an ability to impress others by showing respect, being confident in our abilities, showing leadership in our community, cultivating a positive self-image, speaking in an articulate manner, and being honest and trustworthy. Mrs. Hamilton, our only teacher, demonstrated those characteristics, and we wanted to be just like her!

Most male and female students from the conservative Mennonite community did not progress onto high school since high school was in a nearby town, and the students who attended were a part of "the world" in which the Mennonites were not to participate. Therefore, they were taught at home. The boys learned farming techniques, animal husbandry, and the young ladies learned homemaking skills. Later, the young men might learn a trade such as plumbing, electricity, or carpentry during what was called "Voluntary Service," which they engaged in rather than military service.

In any event, while in the upper grades in our two-room rural school, we were all taught a number of things that our teacher thought would guide us in our lives. Among those were the development of our positive image and the art of positive public relations. We were taught to be kind, considerate, and thoughtful of others in our daily lives. We were taught to develop a manner of behavior that would project a positive public image of our tiny, two-room school and those of us who attended it. We were taught to treat adults with respect, to call them Mr. or Mrs. or Miss when we addressed them (even though we knew all of them by way of our parents), and all in all to project the kind of image of ourselves that would reflect positively on our school and our rural environment.

When one learns that form of behavior in grade school, it tends to carry over into one's adult life. If only our children were taught those behaviors in school today, we might observe a different form of behavior among them. It could become the norm rather than the exception.

HOW DO WE DEVELOP OUR IMAGE—THE DEGREE OF PUBLIC RELATIONS—THAT WE DESIRE?

So, how do we develop our own positive image, and how do we develop the level, or manner, of public relations that will reflect positively not only on us but our own business or our place of employment? Here are a few suggestions:

1. Our image, the level of public relations that we reflect through our daily working lives, is an art. It is an art that is created by each of us. It is our identity; it is who we are in the mind of those we serve each day.

2. Effective and precise communication is essential to the development of a positive image and the level of public relations you desire to develop. The ingredients for that level of communication include, among others, speaking in a precise and confident manner, speaking a little slower than you normally might in order to increase the intelligibility of your speech, presenting what you want to say in the most organized and confident manner, and watching how you present yourself, including your nonverbal manner of communication—how you stand, how you hold yourself, how well controlled your gestures are, and how routinely you make excellent eye contact.

3. Those who communicate well are at a competitive advantage in their professional and social lives. And remember, communication is not optional. Whether we intend to or not, we are still communicating. It is also irreversible. We cannot reverse once we have uttered the

words. We may apologize for saying what we said, but it cannot be taken back. It is, indeed, irreversible.

4. When asked a question, it is important to keep your responses concise and not give more information than was requested.

5. If a client or customer has a concern, always thank the person for expressing the concern. That will set the stage for a more open and positive discussion.

6. Never become emotional, and never get into a shouting match, no matter how close the topic might be to you or how much you feel that you are correct. You will only regret it later.

7. Always keep a sense of humor, and don't expect others to read your mind.

8. Never—never take a cheap shot at a colleague, no matter how good it might make you feel at the moment. You will only regret it later.

9. If someone treats you in an unkind manner, practice forgiving, forgetting, and getting over it.

10. And, always give honest and sincere appreciation for the other person's efforts or opinions.

IN SUMMARY

In order to develop a positive image, remember that the degree of positive influence that will come from the image that you create and the level of positive public relations will depend on the following advice: In all interactions with your colleagues and the public, try always to remain calm, and present yourself with poise, confidence, and as I call it, a touch of "positive vulnerability" that enhances your interpersonal communication and your public image. It is, for lack of another descriptor, the "charm" that persuades and makes others feel at ease. You then become the person with whom others desire to communicate and associate. With that in mind, your positive identity, your level of public relations, and your image will rise to the level you desire.

CHAPTER FIVE

CONTROLLING OUR INFLUENCES

We will either control the influences
around us, or they will control us.
—JIM STOVALL

There are people who influence others one-on-one. These individuals would include mentors, caregivers, and professionals such as lawyers, accountants, or doctors. There are people who influence others in groups such as teachers, scout leaders, or corporate managers. And then there are a few people who have a global influence such as actors, heads of state, or athletes. In much the same way, there are people who have the spotlight of influence for a brief period of time such as Olympic champions, lottery winners, or individuals who act heroically in a crisis; but then there are the rare individuals who have a global influence for a lifetime and beyond.

My late great friend and mentor, Coach John Wooden, was one of these rare and special people. The terms *legendary* and *iconic* are thrown about casually in our society today, and there are very few people who deserve those labels, but John Wooden was one man who did.

After a Hall of Fame college basketball career as a player, he became the head basketball coach of the UCLA Bruins. In a 12-year period spanning the 1960s and 1970s, Coach Wooden's teams had multiple undefeated seasons and won ten national championships. Sports historians and gurus often debate one another regarding which records will never be broken, and virtually all agree that Coach Wooden's coaching records will likely never even be approached.

It's important to understand the magnitude of his accomplishments, as during that era freshmen could not play on the varsity team. So, Coach Wooden blended multiple players together on a number of different teams for more than a decade at a championship level.

I grew up watching Coach Wooden's teams competing each March in the NCAA championships, final four, and national title games. What stood out to me beyond the prowess of his amazing teams and players such as Kareem Abdul-Jabbar and Bill Walton was Coach Wooden's calm demeanor and the total respect his players showed him.

I will never forget the day a colleague came into my office and told me a man named John Wooden was on the phone and wanted to speak with me. Since it is a fairly common name, I, of course, wondered if it was "the" John Wooden. When she explained that he had already ordered several copies of my books and asked that they be autographed and personalized to names such as Kareem Abdul-Jabbar and Bill Walton, among others, I realized I was going to get to talk to one of my boyhood heroes.

At the time of that first conversation, Coach Wooden was 95 years old. You may have heard it said of someone that they had forgotten more than most people ever know. That would have been true of Coach Wooden except I don't think he ever forgot anything.

We had an ongoing dialogue and correspondence over the next several years, and he passed away a few months short of his 100th birthday. Even in our last conversation, I was astounded to hear a 99-year-old man recite long passages of poetry and vividly remember specific games and individual players' performances from more than 50 years in the past.

Coach Wooden may have had his greatest influence after he retired from basketball. He became an author, speaker, and thought leader until the time of his passing.

While the coaching profession is filled with volatile, short-tempered, and often profane individuals, Coach Wooden was the extreme opposite. John Wooden grew up on a farm in the Upper Midwest. As he described it to me, he and his older brother had specific chores and duties around the farm every day. He told me about the time when he was around six years old, and he and his brother, who was approximately nine at the time, were cleaning out the barn. Coach Wooden explained that cleaning out the barn meant removing all the hay and manure from the stalls and replacing it with clean hay.

His brother, as often happens between siblings, decided to play a practical joke on Coach Wooden and tossed a pitchfork full of manure-covered hay onto his younger brother's head. Coach Wooden responded by yelling some profanity he had heard from field hands on the farm just as their father arrived. Coach Wooden remembered his father explaining to him why he should never use that sort of language ever again, and more than 90 years after that incident, Coach Wooden was pleased to report to me he had not.

He believed that if we're going to expect young men playing a game or colleagues doing a job or students in a classroom to act respectfully and honorably, those in a position of influence must model that behavior. He was a big believer in the concept of a leader being a leader all the time, and often reminded his players, "You will be known for a lifetime of great performances or one lapse in judgement."

John Wooden believed that he was more of a teacher than a coach, and his classroom happened to be a basketball court; but he took more pride in his players' performances off the court than on the court. He often updated me about his players who had gone on to become doctors, lawyers, political leaders, scientists, and professors. He was very proud of their children and grandchildren. Coach Wooden's influence on his teams did not stop when they graduated as they stayed in contact with him regularly throughout the remainder of his life.

John Wooden's lasting influence on me is his statement I remember each morning: "Jim, make today your master-piece." This was his way of reminding me and the rest of the world that we can always do better, we have excellence within us, and we must protect our ability to influence others from our own lapses in judgment and behavior.

I encountered Lance Armstrong through my involvement in a professional association within the speaking industry. At the time, he may have been the most recognizable superstar in the world as a result of his multiple Tour de France cycling victories. His speaking fees were astronomical, and he commanded millions of dollars for corporate endorsements.

Then, almost overnight, he was found cheating and caught in a lie to cover up his actions. His positive influence vanished, and his life became a wreck both personally and professionally. The positive influence that he had enjoyed for years instantly became a source of doubts and questions for people who had looked up to Lance Armstrong and what he stood for.

I have long believed in a quote attributed to Gandhi: "Every person is my superior in that I can learn something from them." So, we cannot expect people to be perfect before we can learn from them, but we must remain mindful that our influence is fragile, and in our instant-communication, globally connected world, bad news and harmful information can be disseminated in the blink of an eye.

One of my favorite authors, Louis L'Amour, often stated, "No one can be judged except against the backdrop of the time and place in which they lived." Coach Wooden echoed this sentiment himself when he often repeated, "There's enough bad in the best of us, and enough good in the worst of us, that it doesn't behoove any of us to judge anyone."

While it's true that we should never judge other people, we must carefully select the influences that we allow to impact us. Just because someone is famous or influential does not mean they are worthy to be followed. It could be argued that Adolf Hitler was the most influential person of the 20th century. It could also be argued that he was the most reprehensible person of that century.

Influence is a generic term. It is quite different from defining someone as a positive influence or a valuable influence. Our media-driven culture has created a new brand of fame. There are people today who are famous for simply being famous. There are individuals whose names have become household words, but we would be hard-pressed to cite one accomplishment or achievement in their lives.

If you are ever given a choice between wealth, fame, and character, choose character, and you will have all three. Wealth and fame do not create character, but long-term character often creates wealth and fame.

There are times in life when we want to have more influence for a cause or project than we can bring to it ourselves. I have utilized a concept I call the Dream Team in each of my ventures. This involves calling on people whose experience, expertise, and influence I respect and asking them to become attached to my efforts.

After losing my sight completely at age 29, I found myself broke, scared, and confined to a 9-by-12-foot room in the back of my house. I was afraid to go anywhere and do anything. I really thought I would live the rest of my life in that tiny, self-imposed prison cell. I spent my days sitting in a chair with my radio, telephone, and tape recorder beside me. The thought of traveling millions of miles and speaking to millions of people in arena events, or writing over 40 books with eight of them being turned into movies, or founding and running an Emmy Award-winning television network, or writing a weekly syndicated column read by countless people in newspapers, magazines, and online publications around the world would have seemed as foreign to me as going to the moon.

Thankfully, one of the meager possessions I had in my 9-by-12-foot room was a tape recorder. Several benevolent individuals came to visit me and would occasionally stop by and bring audio books for me to listen to. This is when I got reacquainted with Napoleon Hill through his book *Think and Grow Rich* and was similarly exposed to the thoughts of other great individuals.

Prior to losing my sight, that little 9-by-12-foot room in the back of my house had been our TV room. As a blind person, I knew that somewhere over in the corner, there was a television, a video player, and my collection of classic movies. One day, out of sheer boredom, I put one of those old movies into the video player and turned it on. I thought that I had seen most of the films so many times that I could just listen to the soundtrack and follow the plot.

It turned out that the movie I put into the player was an old Humphrey Bogart film *The Big Sleep*. I listened to the movie for a while and could sort of follow the story to a certain extent from my memory until someone fired a gun, and someone screamed, and a car sped away, and I couldn't remember what was happening. That's when I uttered the magic words: "Somebody ought to do something about that."

The next time you have a challenge or a problem, and you either think or say, "Somebody ought to do something about that," you just had a great idea. Ideas come disguised as problems, and the only thing you need to do to complete the idea is ask yourself, "How could I have avoided that?" The answer is your next big idea. Furthermore, the only thing you have to do to turn your big idea into a business is to ask one more question. "How can I help other people avoid that?" The answer to that question is a great opportunity.

That frustrating moment in my little 9-by-12-foot room was the genesis of what now is the Narrative Television Network. I realized that if we could take standard TV shows, movies, and educational videos and add one extra voice between the existing dialogue to describe the actions, settings, and visual elements of the program, then we could make television and movies accessible to millions of blind and visually impaired people around the world.

While I had a good idea, I didn't have any money, experience, expertise, or contacts. Selling a new concept is always difficult, but introducing something as strange as TV for the blind to the movie and television industry was bizarre. I needed influence that I didn't have, so I decided to create a Dream Team and borrow some other people's influence.

The first person I contacted was Ted Turner. He was an iconic figure in the network TV industry, having created CNN, the Super Station, and a number of other cable services. I wrote to him sharing my hopes, goals, and dreams of how I wanted to improve the lives of millions of blind and visually impaired people, and he agreed to serve on our advisory board. That has been almost 30 years ago, and I still know I can call on Mr. Turner for advice or expertise whenever it is needed.

A blind guy with no experience trying to launch a TV network is laughable. A blind guy with Ted Turner trying to launch a TV network is feasible.

When my books began receiving acceptance and building momentum in the financial services industry, I needed someone with maximum influence to help me spread my message. I reached out to Steve Forbes. He wrote the fore-word to several of my books and remains a friend, mentor, and advisor to this day.

When my novels began drawing interest from the movie industry, I surrounded myself with influential people such as James Garner, Brian Dennehy, Peter Fonda, Michael Landon Jr., Raquel Welch, and Academy Award-winner Louis Gossett Jr. Their credibility gave me the influence I needed to succeed.

Conversely, today, I allow other people to borrow my influence as I serve on the Board of Reference or as an advisor to universities, foundations, charities, and other causes I believe to be important.

Many people think they are the victim of their own anonymity or lack of influence. As we are learning, influence can be created, generated, and even borrowed. It's important to realize that influence is not static. It can be altered, improved, or customized to meet our needs and goals.

CHAPTER SIX

THE INFLUENCE OF CIVILITY AND RESPECT IN THE WORKPLACE

RAY H. HULL, PhD

Lately there has been a flurry of conversation and news on the topic of civility and respect in the workplace. It's a topic that is long overdue for recognition. If we could define the term "civility," it would include the following:

CIVILITY

1. **Civility shows respect toward others**. People are not objects, nor are they simply opportunities for advancement. When we treat others with respect, we are treating them as we would also appreciate being treated. When we are treated with respect, we are shown that we are valued and an important part of a team. We feel free to contribute to the organization in the best way that we can and will not be reprimanded for our efforts if they do not turn out as well as we thought they would. Rather, we will be complimented for our effort.

2. **Civility causes others in the workplace to feel good about being in that environment**. They are being treated with respect, and they are shown that they are valued and that they are an important part of a team. They know that they are in an inclusive work environment where each individual is valued for the

contributions they make to the organization. They know that their superiors work on the basis of facts rather than assumptions or gossip. They know that they are included in decision making and that their contributions to the decision-making process are valued and taken into consideration when final decisions are made.

3. **Civility means that each person in the organization contributes to an atmosphere of mutual respect for others.** Interpersonal communication is an ongoing process with everyone—and that means everyone in the organization, not just those closest to the employer—the boss. Effective interpersonal communication is the key. Those with whom we communicate should feel a connection to us. They should know that we care about them and will support them. People are drawn toward those who make them feel most comfortable, those who communicate with them in a positive and supportive manner. In the end, it is what separates those who are successful in life and in work from those who are less successful.

4. **Civility involves a higher level of communication.** It involves giving honest and sincere appreciation for the work of those in the

organization—and that means everyone, not just your closest colleague or friend at work.

5. **Civility means being a good listener and acknowledging what is important to each person.** We want to recognize what is needed by employees in order to complete a task that is important to them. And they need to know in no uncertain terms that you will help to see that it is achieved—within reason.

6. **Civility means listening with sincere interest to what a colleague/an employee is saying.** We listen carefully, with good eye contact and no side-glances. We concentrate on what the other person is saying, with an occasional nod to assure the person that we are listening. And we never look at our watch! We never interrupt. Rather, we reflect on their feelings with supportive attentiveness and facial expressions. In other words, the employee knows that she or he is respected and valued.

7. **Civility means making sure that the non-verbal aspects of our interactions with others do not purposely or accidentally reflect condescending or insulting connotations.** In other words, it is important to realize that the non-verbal aspects of communication comprise more than 70% of what is being communicated. This means that the words that we use

comprise only about 30% of what is being said. The nonverbal aspects of communication include one's eyes, hands, body language, gestures, vocal inflections, and intonation.

They involve the following:

a. **Remember the two-minute rule**. That means that when an employee or colleague enters your office when called there to meet with you, they will make an appraisal of your attitude, your mood, the intent of the meeting, and your feelings about them within two minutes of entering your office. A smile, a friendly nod, and an outstretched hand to indicate that they are to be seated for a friendly conversation is what they are hoping for. A frustrated frown, a downward look, and a growl for "be seated" and the employee will suddenly drop into survival mode, and expect the worst!

b. **When talking with an employee or colleague in the hallway, remember to keep your distance**. Thirty inches is just fine. No more—no less. Standing too close denotes intimacy that is probably not intended. Too great a distance, the listener may tend to feel devalued.

c. **Your posture while seated is important**. Leaning too far forward, having your shoulders hunched, or slouching indicates that the listener is disengaged from what is being said. Leaning too far back in the chair with a hand covering the mouth indicates hostility toward the talker's ideas or their logic. That may not be intended, but it was communicated on a nonverbal basis. And that is difficult to erase.

d. **Pay attention to your arms and hands**. Arms folded across the chest, especially while standing, can indicate resistance to what is being said. Playing with fingers and nails indicates that you are not really listening to the other person.

e. **Check your eye movements**. Our eyes give us away! Lack of eye contact, or frequent glances to one side or the other indicate serious disagreement, disinterest, or "why am I here?"

Those are all nonverbal aspects of communication that can make or break a conversation with a colleague or employee. When we want them to feel comfortable and know that they are important to us or the organization, the nonverbal aspects of communication are critically important. Being attentive, with an occasional affirmative nod to show that we are listening and interested in what is being said, is comforting to the one who is talking to us. It makes them feel important, respected, and needed.

INCIVILITY IN THE WORKPLACE

So, what is *incivility*? According to Jean Prather, Director of Human Resources, Rose-Hulman Institute of Technology, "Incivility" is defined as:[13]

1. **Social behavior lacking in good manners, including rudeness or behavior that would be interpreted as threatening to another.** I received the following from disgruntled employees of a major industry, wondering what I would do in this instance. The following is the essence of what I heard from them:

I have worked with superiors in two organizations who communicated with me in such a way that I always wished that I hadn't requested an appointment with them. They may not have intended to communicate in that way, but it was what I saw and heard whenever I would walk into their office.

They seemed to be unintentionally rude, as though I was the last person they wanted to see that day. After I had made an appointment to see them and arrived on time, rather than a smile and then saying, "How may I help you, Tom?" or "How are you? Good to see you!" their response to my being there seemed to indicate, "Why are you here?" or "What do ya want?" The intonation of their voice indicated hostility, or at the least that they were irritated about something. Their vocal intonation and facial expression, at the very least, indicated that they were not happy to see me. And, as far as I knew, I had done nothing to irritate them, at least I hoped that I had not done anything wrong. Both of those administrators needed to be talked to about civility in the workplace, or at least talked to about controlling rudeness or otherwise threatening behavior, whether the behavior was intended or unintended.

2. **Condescending language or vocal intonation that degrades another person**. As I said earlier, people value civility. They would like to be treated as they intend to treat others. Sometimes when the workload becomes such that it is irritating or, at least, frustrating, we can become "short" with others. By "short," I mean abrupt, and our tone of voice can become sharp as we give orders to those with whom we are working. It was unintentional, but it happened. The other employee is taken aback at the tone, thinking that we are angry with them. We don't mean to degrade or demean, but it just happened.

That's when we learn that what is communicated is irreversible. All we can do is apologize and move on. An apology is important. If it is not given, the person with whom we were communicating may feel devalued, as though their work is not worthwhile nor, perhaps, are they.

3. **Reprimanding or criticizing someone in front of others**. This is not acceptable behavior, no matter what the cause or the reason. Good behavior in any work environment does not condone reprimanding or criticizing a person in front of other employees, particularly if you are in a supervisory or administrative role or, I should say, any role. Such behavior is not acceptable.

If a mistake is made by an employee, we must do whatever is possible to help that person save face. No matter how wrong or in error we might think the person is, we only destroy their ego and potentially good working relations by embarrassing the other person and hurting their dignity. And hurting someone's dignity can be extremely damaging to an otherwise positive working relationship. By all means, if it is necessary to tell an employee that they made an error and should make a change, the employee's office is the appropriate place to have that conversation. And it must be a private room, not an open concept office cubicle!

4. **Insulting the intelligence of a coworker.** "That is really stupid!" was what I heard an administrator tell a subordinate one day in the hallway of an office complex. The subordinate, the employee, was so embarrassed that she didn't know what to say at the moment. I saw her, red-faced, running down the hallway to her office. She slammed the door, and I heard her sobbing as I walked toward her office to find out what it was all about. However, rather than knocking on her office door, I left her alone until later.

Later, when her office door was open, I gently knocked on the door, and after she acknowledged me standing there, she invited me in. I asked her what that outburst of our administrator was all about. Her eyes began to tear again as she talked. She walked over and closed her office door, and when she came back to where I was standing, she said that she had made a suggestion about the sequence of office hours for the employees that seemed to her to be a more efficient use of our time. She told me that when she went in to talk to him, he didn't even look up or acknowledge her being there. And, when she told him what her suggestion was, he looked up and shouted, "That is really stupid!" and pointed to the door, indicating that she was to leave his office. She had hoped that he would come to see her to apologize for his behavior but had not up to that time.

His behavior was disappointing to say the least. In fact, it was rude and demeaning and was not the behavior one would expect from an administrator in any organization. He should have gone immediately to her office and apologized. If he had had a bad day, or if he had just been told that he had done something "stupid," he might have used that as part of his excuse. But one thing was for sure. He should not expect that employee to feel good about working in that environment, and she probably won't be working as diligently and energetically as she was previously.

5. **Comments or jokes related to gender or sexual issues no matter how innocent they may be to the one making the comments or telling the joke.** This has been a problem during all of the years I have been employed in a public place, sometimes on a rather covert basis and other times on a more overt basis. Nowadays, jokes or comments related to gender or sexual issues have become increasingly accessible by means of social media. It seems

as though I receive items from friends and acquaintances on a weekly basis that appear to be ones that others, including members of both sexes, might find amusing.

However, we have to be very aware that among members of both sexes, issues that we might find amusing may not be amusing to others. In fact, they may find them to be offensive on a religious, moral, or political basis, and definitely not amusing. Even among those who I consider to be my best friends, there are differences of opinion, particularly regarding gender issues and issues of a sexual nature. They may find them to be hilarious, and I find them to be offensive or, at least, not amusing. They expect me to laugh with them, and I cannot. It is not that I am a prude, but there are issues that I hold dear to my heart, particularly those regarding equal rights for women, women's health issues, sex, and others. I do not find "funny" comments or jokes related to those issues to be amusing.

We must realize that in any and all circumstances, those issues should not be circulated within one's office space. They also should not be circulated as email attachments; posted on the internet, on one's door, or any other location where others are exposed to them; nor told to others verbally. I despise it when someone calls me aside and says something akin to, "Hey Ray, want to hear something funny?" And, when I hear it, whether I wanted to or not, the person wonders why I'm not laughing. It is simply not acceptable behavior to expect everyone to find information that is gender specific or sexual in nature to be amusing or desired reading or visual material.

6. **Inappropriately touching someone.** This is an absolute no-no! If someone of the opposite sex is grieving, placing one's arms around them might seem appropriate to you. But to the woman who is grieving, it may not be desired. You have invaded her social space—her personal space. If a person of the opposite sex is grieving and is standing close to you, you might say, "Is there anything I can do?" If she then says, "Yes, you can give me a hug," then consider it appropriate. If a person of the opposite sex is excited and happy about the promotion she has just received, and you say, "Congratulations! Let me give you a hug!" if she opens her arms in preparation for the hug, then you might consider it to be appropriate.

If someone is touching a person of the opposite sex to be amusing or is trying to tease the person by touching them inappropriately, then that is certainly not appropriate behavior and cannot be condoned in any environment! It needs to be reported and dealt with quickly.

7. **Pictures or cartoons posted in the workplace that degrade the opposite sex or are sexually suggestive.** In some environments, such as an army barracks, those have been traditionally seen as part of the norm. In a place of business

or any other environment where people work, study, or meet, such postings are not appropriate and should not be condoned! Enough said on that topic.

8. **Promoting cultural or gender bias in the workplace.** In any place of business or service, this has not been permitted for a number of years now, or at least it has been frowned upon. If any indication of this is discovered in any place of business or service, then it should be reported. However, such bias may be subversive in nature and not really observable unless the roster of employees is studied. And then, such bias may be discovered. And gender bias can be called by another name. That name is discrimination on the basis of gender. At the university where I am principally employed, no discrimination is allowed based on gender, race, ethnicity, sexual orientation, military status, age, and so on. Absolutely no bias or discrimination is permitted in the employment of faculty, administrators, or staff—ever.

THE RESULT?

The result of a lack of respect and civil behavior toward others in the close confines of a work environment, particularly if those behaviors originate from the employer, one's immediate superior, or close colleagues, usually results in employees who are fearful and stressed on the job. Therefore, they don't perform their responsibilities to their potential. In a study published in the *Journal of Occupational Health Psychology*, in a survey of 1100 workers, 781 had experienced workplace incivility.[14] According to S. Chris Edmonds in "The Little Black Book of Billionaire Secrets," which appeared in the *Forbes Community Voice* in 2016, 62% of employees had been treated rudely at work at least once a month. The rudeness had come from coworkers and/or their superiors.[15]

Again, in that type of work environment, employees do not perform to their best ability. They feel degraded and will generally not perform at a level they are capable of performing. They will simply "do their job" and leave as a less productive employee at the end of the day. The cost of reduced commitment to their place of employment as a result of anxiety and decreased effort can be extremely high.

HOW CAN CIVILITY AND RESPECT IN THE WORKPLACE BE ENCOURAGED?

Here are some suggestions:

1. **We must be an important part of the atmosphere that promotes respect and civility.** We can be the one who demonstrates respect and civility to others every day. We can consider that one of our responsibilities within the workplace environment because it is important for the morale of those who work in our place of employment. We can be the example

of one who values the contributions of those who work with us. We can compliment and congratulate others when they achieve a goal or accomplish a significant task. However, in the meantime, we must not denigrate ourselves by lowering the significance of our own accomplishments. But perhaps in congratulating others for their good work or their accomplishments, they will in turn compliment us when we accomplish a significant task or receive an award. Comradery within the workplace is the goal, and it is refreshing.

2. **If employees are covertly or overtly disrespectful of others in their workplace, we must deal with it immediately rather than wait to see if they will change their behaviors.** Most people who are disrespectful of others on either a covert or overt level will not change on their own, primarily because either they cannot see anything wrong with their behavior, or they believe that others in their work environment deserve that behavior. If you find yourself the brunt of that form of behavior, you can deal with it in one of two ways. One way is you can inform your superior of the behavior, and have instances documented for proof since it is easy for the perpetrator to simply deny doing anything. Another way of dealing with that type of behavior is to confront the

disrespectful person, tell them that you do not appreciate what they have said or done to you, and in a tone of voice that is convincing, say, "And please do not do it again. It has been going on much too long!" If the person retaliates in some way, then it is appropriate to go to your superior and discuss the issue.

3. **All employees must meet as a group and discuss the nature of respect and civility in the workplace rather than wait until bad behavior is obvious and then meet to stop it.** That is an appropriate measure to take in any organization. As Barney Fife in the old Andy Griffith show would say, "Nip it in the bud! Nip it—nip it—nip it!" Take care of issues before it becomes necessary to confront them. A special group meeting that discusses workplace civility and respect at the beginning of the year is quite appropriate. It is appropriate at such a meeting to assure the employees that the meeting is being held to raise awareness and to encourage comradery in the organization rather than to reprimand. You might say, "We are all here together to work together, to support each other, to congratulate each other when something has been done well or someone has received an award, to respect each other, and to work in a positive and supportive environment." That would be the essence

of the meeting and, hopefully, will be enough said on the topic.

4. **We must emphasize to all employees, no matter what level within the organizational structure, that appropriateness in behavior is essential, and that inappropriate behavior will be dealt with severely.** It should be emphasized that no off-color jokes or remarks, no matter how innocent they appear to the person who uttered them, will be tolerated, and any inappropriate or unwanted touching, no matter how innocent it appears to the person who engaged in it, will be dealt with appropriately.

In the end, people value respect and civility. Most people desire to treat others as they would like to be treated. However, occurrences of incivility do happen in any workplace. An occasional outburst of frustration can be absorbed in a healthy work environment. It can be overlooked as a result of an overworked colleague. We realize that no one is perfect, and we can continue to love and value our colleague in spite of the outburst.

CHAPTER SEVEN

ON-PURPOSE
INFLUENCING

*Our influence is the impact of
our personality and performance
on the world around us.*
—JIM STOVALL

O ur influence does not create us, but instead, we craft our influence and create it. Our influence can be flexible and variable depending upon our situation or short-term goals.

Recently, I read a new biography of Leonardo da Vinci. Leonardo may have been the most influential person of all time. He was renowned in multiple circles and areas of expertise. In a letter he wrote to a government official seeking a sponsorship for his work, Leonardo described his talents, experience, and influence in the fields of anatomy, botany, engineering, weaponry, music, design, astronomy, and a number of other pursuits. In the eleventh paragraph of that letter, he wrote, "...and I paint."

It is a testament to Leonardo da Vinci's influence in a broad spectrum of endeavors that the most famous painter of his era—and possibly of all time—could describe himself as having influence in a multitude of fields before he even mentioned himself as an artist.

Many people know Ted Williams as possibly the greatest baseball hitter of all time, but they may not be aware that he was also a champion sports fisherman and a decorated fighter pilot during World War II.

Benjamin Franklin may be the American with the most diverse influence in our nation's history. He was a publisher, a scientist, a philosopher, and an inventor, but if you only remember him as influential in those areas, you're overlooking his influence in the founding of America and the concept of freedom that continues to spread around the world.

One of the hardest questions I am ever asked is, "What do you do?" I can break my professional life down into five areas: books, television, movies, speeches, and columns. I believe I have a certain degree of influence in all these fields, and I endeavor to build one atop the other. I have a tendency to think of the five elements of my work like a four-sided pyramid with a point on the top. The point is whichever element I'm working on at the moment, but it must support and be supported by the other four.

As I am dictating the words you are reading in this book, I will introduce and cross-promote the other elements of my professional life in mutually beneficial ways. This book will be promoted through my columns, speeches, and television work. The movies based on my novels are narrated for the blind and visually impaired audience we serve at the Narrative Television Network.

If you're going to have a multi-pronged, diverse professional life, craft your influence to serve all your endeavors. This concept should be considered before you launch a project.

The concept of line extension in the corporate world has created a lot of popular buzz, but it is overutilized. If a popular potato chip company wants to extend their line and influence into the popcorn or tortilla market, it may be valid, but if the same successful potato chip company wants to start manufacturing and marketing snow tires, it is absurd. Their influence may cross over within the snack aisle at your grocery store but doesn't extend to your local automotive center.

Just as your influence can be shaped and extended, it can be repaired and rehabilitated.

In 1913, Richard Nixon was born into a relatively average, middle-class family. Through sheer tenacity and dogged persistence, he distinguished himself academically, in the military, and throughout his political career. In 1968, he was elected president, and re-elected for a second term in 1972. But then, due to a ridiculous botched burglary and the ensuing cover-up, he was forced to resign the presidency.

At the point President Nixon left the White House in shame, it would be hard to imagine a more maligned and defeated person. He had been one of the most influential people on the earth and had fallen to a point of disgrace and ridicule; but then, through another persistent effort over many years, Mr. Nixon began to rehabilitate his image and his influence. While he never escaped the stain of Watergate throughout his life or in his legacy, by the time of his death in 1994, he was a respected elder statesman of sorts, particularly with respect to foreign affairs and diplomacy.

His book, *In the Arena / A Story of Victory, Defeat, and Renewal*, is a great example of how influence can be created, lost, reengineered, and regained.

Whether you are in poverty, in prison, or dealing with any of life's challenges, the thing that is limiting your influence now can actually extend your influence once you achieve a degree of success.

As a blind person myself, confined to a 9-by-12-foot room in the back of my house, I had virtually zero influence. Today, the fact that I am blind when added to the fact that I am a bestselling author, movie producer, entrepreneur, and self-made multimillionaire gives me greater credibility and broader influence.

The extent of a person's legacy of influence cannot be judged in a moment of time like a snapshot. It must play out for a long period like an epic movie.

I remember hearing the news reports coming in from around the world when Princess Diana passed away. It was a tragedy that captured the attention of the media and the whole world. Several days later, as Diana's funeral was being televised, a few news stories surfaced reporting that Mother Teresa had died. Mother Teresa's media coverage of her passing was totally dwarfed and overwhelmed by the media event surrounding Diana's funeral.

While Diana and Mother Teresa were both influential figures, and even though Diana's influence and popularity seemed greater than Mother Teresa's at the time of their deaths, I feel certain that history will record the immense contribution that Mother Teresa made throughout her life as well as her lasting legacy of service in a way that will far supersede how history will view Diana. Popularity is a fleeting image while influence and legacy represent the true impact and value of an individual.

Our influence is greatly impacted by our habits. When a person is known over a long period of time as never doing something bad or always doing something good, their habit creates a stronger influence.

I have been very fortunate to have some significant people show up at the right time throughout my professional life and in a number of my projects. I never really intended to be an author, but during a speaking tour to promote Narrative Television Network, two of my fellow speakers on the program—Dr. Robert Schuller and Dr. Denis Waitley—strongly encouraged me to write a book. I finally agreed and told my story of losing my sight and building my business career in a book that was titled *You Don't Have to be Blind to See.*

It was well-received, so the publisher asked me to write a second book, then a third, and so on. After my seventh title, when they requested another book, I realized I had written everything I knew and a few things I only suspected, so I decided to make up a story and write a novel.

Over the next five days in my office at the Narrative Television Network, between my meetings and calls, I dictated *The Ultimate Gift.* There were never any edits or rewrites to that manuscript. The way I dictated it to my able colleague Dorothy Thompson is the way millions of people around the world read that book.

The Ultimate Gift was so popular, I had several studios that wanted to turn the story into a movie.

The first studio wanted to turn my family-oriented, message-based novel into an R-rated movie. While in principle I don't have any problem with films like *Saving Private Ryan* or *Schindler's List* being R-rated, to take my story which is used in hundreds of schools as part of their curriculum and turn it into an R-rated film that the students couldn't even go see in their local theatre seemed absurd to me; so with great fear and trepidation, I turned the studio's offer down, thinking there would never be an *Ultimate Gift* movie.

It wasn't long until a second and even a third offer emerged, and eventually I agreed to work with a talented movie producer named Rick Eldridge who has become a great colleague and friend throughout a number of movie projects on which we have collaborated.

One of the greatest days of my professional life was when James Garner agreed to play the role of my lead character in *The Ultimate Gift*, Red Stevens. Mr. Garner had an amazing film and television career spanning more than half a century.

During that time, as he explained it to me, he played parts in a number of projects involving war, crime, the Wild West, and detectives, but he never, in any of his roles, would agree to shoot anyone with a gun. While his anti-violence stance may have cost him a few parts throughout the years, over time, it created an amazing influence for him within the industry and is a lasting part of his legacy.

In the third movie in *The Ultimate Gift* trilogy, Raquel Welch brought my iconic character Sally Mae Anderson to life on the screen. Miss Welch, while obviously being one of the most beautiful and well-known actresses of her era, made a commitment early in her career to never take any parts that involved nudity or exploitive sexuality. As she explained to me, those kinds of parts would have made her a lot of money in the short run and limited her career in the long run. She went on to say, "I would never have had the chance to do your movie, *The Ultimate Legacy*, if I had that kind of reputation."

In many cases, accepting less or delayed success in the short term can heighten your influence and success for the rest of your life and beyond.

When you use your influence to deliver a message, it is important that you are sure that the message you're sending is the message that others are receiving. Just because you're talking doesn't mean anyone's listening; and even if they are listening, it doesn't mean they understand; and even if they understand, it doesn't mean they're receiving the same message you mean to send.

Shortly after losing my sight, I received a white cane and several months of mobility training in how to use it. When I finally ventured out of my 9-by-12-foot room, my white cane and I were able to travel two blocks down the sidewalk to a park near where I lived at that time. After being stuck in a small room in the back of my house for months, it was nice to sit on a bench in the park, feel the breeze and sun on my face, and enjoy the sounds of children playing, ballgames, and all the other activity in the park.

I remember the day when a young boy and his father were sitting on the bench next to me. The boy had obviously received a puppy, and Dad had determined it was time to get this dog some training; so as I was able to interpret the sounds, the father threw a ball quite a distance from where we were seated. Then he told his son to let the dog go fetch it.

The dog rushed through the grass and did, indeed, pick up the ball, but instead of bringing it back, he proceeded to run throughout the park exploring everything that was going on in the area. The father yelled and whistled, but the dog paid no attention. The young boy began crying, thinking he may have lost his dog, but eventually, the dog returned and flopped down on the grass between the father and son, totally exhausted from his adventures running through the park.

The father immediately grabbed a rolled-up newspaper and began beating the dog while admonishing it to never run away again. The young boy cried uncontrollably watching his father hit his new dog. Finally, the father realized his son was in emotional distress and tried to offer an explanation saying, "We have to discipline him so he will learn his lesson." Then the father asked his son, "Do you understand what we're teaching the dog?"

The boy confidently responded, "Yes. We're teaching my dog that when he finally understands what you want him to do and comes back to us, you hit him with a newspaper."

Images reinforce messages, and messages are the fuel of our influence, but we always have to be sure it's well-crafted and properly directed.

A picture can be worth much more than a thousand words in the way it influences people. Who could ever forget the vivid images of the World Trade Center collapsing on September 11th? No vivid description or creative words could ever capture that imagery.

One of the most emotionally impactful experiences I have ever had was my visit to the Holocaust Museum in Washington, DC. I wasn't sure what to expect, but above the door where I entered the museum was a sign that read, "May we never forget." Then as I entered the museum, I was at one end of a long hall which was lined on both sides by shoes extending the entire length of the hall. Remembering the stories of prisoners being killed with poison gas in the showers, that long line of empty shoes influenced me in a way I will never forget.

Our influence is more than our words and our attitudes. It extends to the tools we can use to create life-changing images.

CHAPTER EIGHT

THE INFLUENCE OF LEARNING: LEARNING THAT INFLUENCES US THROUGHOUT OUR LIVES

RAY H. HULL, PhD

In thinking about the concept of "learning" and how it influences us throughout our lives, I cannot help but recall my early learning experiences that I gained while at the rural school I attended through the eighth grade. When I first began my education in that very small, two-room school, I had just been transferred from an elementary school in town. The school that I attended in town was a cultural shock after my quiet life on the farm where I had lived since birth. Playground fights were rather routine. As a child with a severe stuttering problem, I was picked on regularly, laughed at, and regularly called names. I was miserable. Plus my third grade teacher was merciless. She seemed to enjoy making children feel inadequate.

When I was taken from that environment and enrolled in the new, tiny, two-room rural school that my father had helped found, the environment was quite different. Most of the other students were from a very conservative Mennonite community, where my family also farmed, and were kind, gentle, and warm in their response to me. Even though I was a child from a family who was "of the world" (as they called us since we were not of the Mennonite faith and heritage) and of a different religious faith, I was still treated with respect and kindness.

The school had two classrooms. One was the "upper-class room" which meant it was for students in the fifth, sixth, seventh, and eighth grades. The "lower-class room" contained grades one, two, three, and four. Each room had their own teacher—one teacher for four grades in each of the two classrooms. Each individual row of students was a "class." So in the upper room, there were four rows of students, one for each grade. When I started attending that school, called "Harmony School," there were three of us in the fourth grade, two girls and myself. The environment was so different from that to which I had become accustomed in "town school" that it took me a while to learn about the new environment and *learn how to learn* in that new school.

As students advanced through the grades, the only thing that identified one's advancement was that one's current grade was moved into a row that was one row closer to the windows on the north side of the room nearest the highway. As we studied our lessons each day, it was interesting to hear the recitations from the other students as they presented what they had learned, whether the lesson was history, mathematics, social studies, or spelling. It took a while for me to adjust to hearing what the grades above me had learned, listening to their recitations through one ear, and also concentrating on what I was studying for my lessons.

Since most of the children were of a conservative Mennonite order, their schooling ended at the eighth grade. At that time, they graduated by way of a formal graduation ceremony in a nearby community and then went on with their life. They were not allowed to go on to high school since that was considered by their community and their church as being "of the world," the world they were not to be exposed to.

These were gentle and nurturing children who I liked very much. The girls wore long print dresses, dark hose, plain shoes, and their hair was tightly braided under their white cap that had long straps that hung loosely around their shoulders. The boys wore blue jeans or rather loose, obviously homemade pants held in place with suspenders, high-top shoes, high-buttoned shirts, and a standard flat-brimmed hat—either brown or black.

Since one teacher taught four different grades in each of the two classrooms, during four years we got to know her pretty well. And, since the lowest grade in each classroom heard all of the lessons of the higher grades each day, by the time you reached the upper grades in that same classroom, you had experienced all of their lessons for two or three consecutive years, so you knew them nearly by heart by the time it was your turn! So, one progressed through the grades with greater speed than in a typical school.

WHAT I LEARNED FROM MY TEACHER, MRS. HAMILTON

In the book by Jim Stovall and myself entitled *The Art of Learning* that was published by Sound Wisdom Publishing and released in 2017, I describe my teacher, Mrs. Hamilton.[16] She was the personification of "learning", since she influenced her students in positive ways that lasted throughout their lives.

Mrs. Hamilton was my teacher at my two-room country school. In her classroom were four grades—the fifth, sixth, seventh, and eighth grades. There were three of us in my fourth grade class, and upon graduating from fourth grade, we moved on into the second classroom where Mrs. Hamilton was the teacher, and entered the fifth grade.

She went much beyond "teaching" and engrained within her students the sheer wonder of learning—that learning went much beyond the classroom and textbooks. Learning was about touching, seeing, and hearing the wonders of the world. Learning was demonstrated to us as something that extended beyond a classroom into the majesty of all that was around us. She taught us to wonder, to imagine, to dream, to feel, to venture into the unknown.

I think that all students have a favorite teacher at sometime within their years of schooling. Well, Mrs. Hamilton was mine—my favorite. She was wonderful! She not only taught us what was in our textbooks, but she taught us much beyond that. We learned about the world; we learned about things we had never seen, things that went beyond our classroom activities and textbook-learning experiences.

Mrs. Hamilton taught us to go beyond our country school, to learn about the world beyond that rather remote location. She brought us seashells from Hawaii; she brought us a pomegranate to taste; she brought us souvenirs from Mexico; she gave each of us a jar of earth and a seed and asked us to plant it in the dirt in the jar, water it, and sit it by the schoolhouse window so we could see the roots begin to grow and then the plant emerge from the earth as the leaves would begin to stretch forth; and many more experiences about the world.

Mrs. Hamilton taught us to go beyond our textbooks, and learn about many things. Mrs. Hamilton probably wasn't thinking about those experiences in this way, but in one way or another, she was preparing the children in her classroom to become lifelong learners, to continue to explore the world, and to learn in ways that would influence them throughout their lives!

When I completed fourth grade in the lower class room and graduated into the upper-class room, that move transformed my life. I never did know her first name. I just knew her as Mrs. Hamilton. She wasn't beautiful, but she was pretty in a pleasant sort of way, and I thought she was absolutely wonderful! Through her, we learned more than the academic subjects that were required of her to teach, and her influence has remained with me through these many years. Of all the many things I learned from her, I remember these to this day:

1. We learned academic honesty and integrity.

2. We learned about table etiquette when we began having hot lunches in the basement of our two room school:

   a. Where the silverware was to be placed on the table.

   b. To seat the young lady next to you.

   c. To engage in appropriate dinner conversation.

   d. To always be polite, and to ask that food be passed rather than reach for it.

Those were all important learning experiences for children who were born and raised on farms in the middle of Kansas. Some of us had been taught many of those at home, but some apparently not.

One day, she brought seashells from Hawaii that she had picked from the beach while on a vacation. Most of us had never seen such pretty shells before, nor even imagined them from our rather isolated vantage point on farms in the middle of rural Kansas. Had we even thought about Hawaii, it would have been through our World Geography book. Hawaii seemed like a very distant and very exotic place to be seen only through pictures.

She brought fruits and vegetables that many of us had never seen nor tasted before, including pomegranate, papaya, mango, bok choy, and others. And we all had the opportunity to taste them. Having experienced primarily basic nutrition grown on our farms or bought at the grocery store in our nearby town, we had never experienced such exotic tastes before, but we learned something new during those experiences with Mrs. Hamilton.

We learned about strict discipline in the classroom—that is, no whispering, no squirming, no turning around to look at the person behind us. However, no matter how strict the discipline, we learned that it could be administered with love and compassion.

We learned each day that she loved every one of us, no matter how smelly we were from doing farm chores before coming to school, wearing our smelly shoes, and usually only bathing once per week. By Friday, I imagine that many of us were fairly ripe!

We learned from her how to play fairly on the playground, which was simply an open field behind our school.

We continued to learn from Mrs. Hamilton even at the lunch table. At lunchtime, when we began to have hot lunches at school, all of us sat around one long table in the basement of our school. With Mrs. Hamilton seated at the head of the table, she would have us all bow our heads as she led us in a prayer of thanks before we ate.

One year, our school received many large sacks of Government Surplus white beans. So for one full academic year, we ate white beans, mashed potatoes with white gravy, and corn bread for lunch quite frequently. And, even in spite of the regularity of white beans and corn bread, the prayer of thanks was said each day. Ladies who wore long cotton print dresses, dark hose, plain shoes, with their hair pulled tightly under their black or dark blue Mennonite caps were our cooks. The white gravy that they made was from just flour, water, and salt. Compared to the rich cream gravy that my mother made at home, it tasted absolutely awful. However, we learned not to tell the cooks how awful it tasted. But rather, we learned to thank them pleasantly for their work on our behalf.

On certain days when we were to bring our own sack lunches or a lunch pail because there was to be no hot lunch downstairs in the school basement, we ate quietly at our desks in our classroom. Mrs. Hamilton would sit at her desk while nibbling at her own lunch and would read us stories written by Laura Ingles Wilder from the *Little House on the Prairie* books. We learned many things from those stories. We learned about the life of a family living on the prairie, about survival in a terrible snow storm, about Native Americans, and other things. Those times were special to all of us. When she read, she read in such a way that it almost seemed as though we were there with the Wilder family in that long winter! And, rather than simply ending each story, we continued learning as we talked about what we had heard and learned from what she had read to us.

Mrs. Hamilton is the one teacher I have remembered throughout the years. The others I have forgotten, except for the bad ones. I think about her from time to time, and I am sure that she has passed on by now. She was strict, but we knew that she loved us all. We were safe, nurtured, and not only learned our subjects well, but learned many other valuable lessons about life, about being considerate of others, about love, about treating others with respect, about being tolerant of differences in others, and many other lessons through her.

And, rather than trying to find fault, she praised us for the good work that we accomplished in school. To me, she was a breath of fresh air that encouraged me to learn and to enjoy the process of learning each day.

THIS IS HOW WE LEARN

Research has repeatedly shown that we learn in many different ways. As children develop, they form new ways of representing their world. Each child develops their own "world model," which is their own personal concept of the world, the world from which they would venture forth into new avenues of learning.

My world was very different from that of my acquaintances who lived in the town or in the city. My world centered on open spaces in the country, including my "hiding place" out in the grove of trees about 100 yards north of our farm house next to the pasture where our dairy cows lounged and grazed each day. The hayloft above our large wooden barn where I would play in the hay, watch a bobcat that had taken up residence there one winter, and where I could think about life and make up games to play. My world model included getting my calf ready to show at the 4-H Fair in the summer, grieving over a dead cow, watching a baby calf being born, and then observing him or her searching for nourishment from his or her mother immediately after birth. Then, as I grew in age and strength, I was given responsibilities that involved work around the farm.

The "world model" of my acquaintances who lived in town seemed to be quite different, more confined to small yards, play that was inside their house, riding their bicycle on smooth streets and sidewalks rather than on rough gravel and sand roads that I had to try to negotiate, playing with friends who lived nearby, getting into fights over issues that seemed to be major ones at the time, going to the drugstore for a soda, and others that to my way of thinking were from a different world and not of mine. Occasionally I envied them. But most of the time I didn't.

WE MUST WANT TO LEARN

But, in order to become a learner, one has to either want to learn or have a reason for learning—the learner must be inspired to learn. In one way or another, one must *want* to learn. In my country school, learning seemed to come very naturally. However, we also had to learn the subject matter that we were supposed to learn in accordance with the academic standards of our State Department of Education. Those subjects I learned because it was required of us. But Mrs. Hamilton encouraged us, and she rewarded us with praise when we did well. We—well, at least I—wanted to do well for her. I wanted her to be proud of me.

But, for the average learner to want to learn new information, the subject must be interesting. That is particularly important for adult learners who are learning as a part of self-development. That form of learning is called *intentional learning*. Whether an intentional learner happened to see a segment on television about snow skiing, or fly fishing, or learning to play the accordion, or for the math enthusiast, learning a new form of mathematical calculation, a spark of interest to learn more about the subject may have been lit. So, going to the local library, or the video store, or to Google to find out more about the subject may be the next step.

In the book *The Art of Learning* by Jim Stovall and myself, I refer to a friend of mine who, while seated in her dentist's office waiting room, happened to see a segment in *National Geographic* that showed beautiful photographs of scenery and people. Those photographs so intrigued her that she started looking for books on photography. She became an avid reader on that subject to the extent that she went to a camera store and bought a good camera and some lenses that would allow for some photographic creations that she wanted to try. She then enrolled in a course on photography at a local community college and began taking evening classes on that subject that included scenic and professional photography of people. She even started developing her own photographs in a dark room that she created in the basement of her home.

As a result of the extensive reading that she continued to engage in on the subject of photography and the formal courses that she was taking, she eventually decided on a part-time career change to professional photography. She seemed to have a knack for taking excellent photographs of people, so she leased a space in a strip mall and opened a small photography studio with the intent of doing portrait photography on a part-time basis. In light of her learned skill in photographing scenery and people, she became a sought-after photographer for weddings, graduations, and other events that combined the use of outdoor scenery and excellent portrait photography of people of all ages.

So, *intentional learning* for this woman paid off in a successful career in photography! I didn't become a professional tap dancer, although I enrolled in tap dance instruction because I wanted to improve my skill in that form of dance. As I improved my skills, during high school and college, I was sought after as a dance performer for stage productions with small groups of dancers and was a member of a dance team that performed for many occasions, particularly in college. I wasn't a professional performer, but I had fun and made a little money for various performances!

THERE ARE SO MANY THEORIES OF LEARNING

There are so many theories of learning—some traditional, others that seem logical in their approach, and others that we hear little about. For example, there is some discussion about whether it is best to learn in group environments or individually. As I said in the book *The Art of Learning*, I don't do well in group learning environments—too much discussion, too much competiveness, and too many distractions. However, I was reading the other day about a theory of learning called the *Collaborative Learning Model*. The title of the article was "Supporting Social Interaction in an Intelligent Collaborative Learning System" by Amy Soller. As I read that article, it led me to remembering one of my significant learning experiences.[17]

It is a model of learning that I can identify with. When I was in college, the young lady to whom I was most attracted was an excellent student. I thought that she was not only beautiful, but she was intelligent, outgoing, and the model of student her professors wished everyone would be. Up to that time, I had been, to say the least, an average student. I studied only what I felt I had to study and spent more time being in plays and musicals than in the classroom. The young lady who I sought after seemed to not even be aware that I existed, let alone be a young man to whom she might be attracted.

As time passed, realizing more and more that I was making no progress in getting her interested in me, I began to think that perhaps if I was more like her, a star student, maybe she would be more attracted to me. So, I began to study harder. My time in the library was taken seriously, and my reason for being there went beyond "girl watching" to actually learning the material for the courses I was taking that semester. I began to become known as a serious student. I even asked the young lady who was the impetus for the change in my attitude if we could study together from time to time. And to my surprise, she said, "Yes." And after a while, our Wednesday evening study time became a regular event!

If one is looking for an example of the Collaborative Learning Model, I suppose that the previous story is one of those. Of course, there are other examples that could have been shared, but that one has a happy outcome!

SO, HOW DOES LEARNING INFLUENCE US ?

First of all, one must *want* to learn. If learning is to be influential in our life, the subject must be interesting to us so we will *want* to learn.

At a young age, I learned to tap dance and practiced on the concrete floor of my father's milk barn on our farm. That good, loud tapping sound that was generated on that concrete floor as it echoed within an empty barn was truly reinforcing. As I took lessons and learned more about technique, I became better and better at that form of dance. I didn't become a professional tap dancer, and I wasn't an absolutely great performer like my idol Gene Kelly in the movie *Singing in the Rain*, but I had fun and made a little money for various performances! And it was fun to continue to learn and refine my abilities in that form of dance. The reason was that I wanted to learn more. I wanted to become better.

LEARNING DOESN'T HAVE TO BE INTENTIONAL. IT CAN HAPPEN ANYWHERE.

As I said earlier, I grew up on a farm in the center of Kansas. You cannot find a more stereotypical rural setting than that. I was born and raised there in that 120-year-old farm house and was there throughout all of my years of schooling, including college and some of my years of graduate school.

Between college and graduate school, I was responsible for three of our hired hands in one way or another, making sure they were fulfilling their responsibilities and giving them their duties each day. Their names were Elmer Mowbray, A.P. Nichols, and Slim Elder. These three are described earlier in the book by Jim Stovall and myself *The Art of Learning and Self-Development*.

Elmer Mowbray was an older man who typically had a very used, unlit cigar tucked away in the corner of his mouth. He walked slowly, talked slowly, seemed to think slowly, but he was always on the job ready to lend a hand. We could always depend on Elmer to be there when we needed help with fence repairs, driving the tractor to pull a hay wagon to pick up hay bales out in the field, or other such chores.

A. P. Nichols was also an older man—small in stature, talked softly, never married, and lived with his sister on a neighboring farm. He worked around our farm when we needed extra help. He was a kind and gentle soul who never had a harsh word to say about anyone. Both he and Elmer had solid philosophies of life that they would tell me about from time to time. If I had a question about life, love, or sin, all I had to do was ask, and they would expound on their philosophy about it. I learned a great deal from these two men mostly in an unintentional way. All I had to do was ask a question about something that might have been concerning me, and I would receive their thoughts on the matter.

One day, at about age 14, while all three of us were sitting on top of five layers of hay bales on a hay wagon as it was being pulled by my father who was driving one of our tractors toward the hayloft where those bales were to be stacked, I asked both of them what they thought about God. The response by A.P. and Elmer, almost simultaneously, was, "That's something that we don't have to worry about. God is with us throughout every day and night of our lives. He loves us and will take us to Heaven when we die." That was it—a matter of fact response that to them needed no discussion. Nothing else was mentioned. I have remembered that conversation to this day.

Slim Elder was another matter. I was never quite sure of his age, but he was probably around 30 years old, thin as a rail, and much taller than I was. He spoke with a slow Kansas drawl and usually had a cigarette tucked away on top of one of his ears. One day when I was 16 years of age, as we were sitting in the shade by one of our out-buildings on the farm waiting for a load of wheat to be brought in so we could shovel it into one of our many grain bins, I asked him if he had a girlfriend and if he knew anything about love. He perked up and said without hesitation, "Sure I have a girlfriend. She lives over by Windom (Kansas). I see her every once in a while. We're sort of going steady. Why?"

I told him that I had been dating a young lady, a Mennonite girl, and liked her a lot. I said that it feels like "love," but I don't know what love is. All Slim said was, "When it's love, you'll know it." So, then I asked him, "How will I know it?" Slim's only reply was, "That's it. You'll know it. It's a special feeling that will tell you that it is love." That ended the conversation. I pondered what he said for some time, but all I could do was believe him. I'm not sure if he really knew what love was or if he was ever in love. But I believed him. After all, he was around 30 years of age, so he should know.

Those were learning experiences that happened on a hay wagon and in the shade of an outbuilding on one of our farms. They didn't happen in a classroom, or from a book, or even on Google. But they were still good learning experiences that came from good, honest people, and they happen once in a lifetime.

That is what learning is all about!

CHAPTER NINE

INSTRUMENTS OF
INFLUENCE

*Communication, media, and commerce
are tools we use to leverage our influence.*
—JIM STOVALL

There are a myriad of books, instructional videos, courses, and seminars designed to help people create a success image. Everything from "dress for success" to "fake it until you make it" are concepts that are intended to improve your image and your influence. While I am a big believer in putting yourself and your efforts in the best light possible, in the final analysis, truth will govern your influence.

When I first began my business career, I was fortunate to get an eminent attorney to represent me. He was fond of saying, "Let's assume that the truth will ultimately be known."

My coauthor, colleagues, publishers, and I have endeavored to make this a quality book. From the design of the cover to the proofreading and editing of the text, a number of talented individuals have worked diligently to make this book the best it can be, but if this title proves to be as influential as Dr. Hull and I intend it to be, it will be a result of the content and thoughts, not the external imagery.

Obviously, if you have great content but have a poor cover and text that is filled with typographical errors, it can damage a book's influence; but the greatest, most artistic cover of all time coupled with a flawless, perfectly edited text cannot overcome a weak or invalid message. People do, indeed, judge a book by its cover but only until they open the book and begin to read it. Then the message determines how influential it will be.

The best way I know to protect, develop, and build your influence is to be truly influential in ways that matter to the greatest number of people.

When I first met my mentor, Lee Braxton, and asked him for the key to success, he responded without hesitating, "Always do what you say you're going to do." I was looking for some hidden trick or unknown secret to generating millions of dollars, and that little old man was giving me what I thought was some kind of platitude or Pollyanna. When I look back at his words through the lens of experience and hindsight, I now realize that always doing what you say you're going to do is the best way to succeed and create a lasting legacy of influence.

As we have discussed in a previous chapter, you should never take advice from anyone who doesn't have what you want. There's a myriad of people wanting to influence you by selling their advice via books, cable TV infomercials, and seminars. These people may look good at first glance, but most times a deeper examination will reveal they have created an image of smoke and mirrors that will not stand the test of time.

Unfortunately, if you don't perform your own due diligence checking these people out, they can influence you in destructive and damaging ways. Not only can they take your money, but more significantly, they can waste your time, energy, and passion. Being known as a person whose word is good and delivers what is promised is the foundation of a powerful influence.

The best way to look successful is to, quite simply, be successful. When I wrote my book *The Millionaire Map* telling readers how to achieve wealth and prosperity, I felt they were entitled to know beyond a shadow of a doubt that they were dealing with someone who had been where they wanted to go. With that in mind, I had to do something that was somewhat uncomfortable. I had Merrill Lynch and Bank of America create a financial statement of my holdings excluding my businesses, real estate, and book and movie royalties. This statement assured my readers that just my investment portfolio was worth in excess of $10 million.

As I dictate these words you are reading, it is still difficult to make that kind of a statement because in our culture we are taught that it is not polite or proper to discuss money, sex, or religion. I'm grateful that this book does not deal with sex and religion, or I would feel compelled to provide you of evidence of my expertise and knowledge in those areas.

Realizing that if we are going to be influential leaders, we must be successful people worthy of being followed. Success creates its own level of influence. All of us want to succeed at whatever passion we are pursuing in our lives.

I hate to be the one to give you the bad news, but life isn't fair. It's great, it's grand, and it's wonderful, but it's not fair. We don't all start at the same place. Some of us are in debt, some of us have disabilities, while others come from challenging backgrounds, but we can all reach our goals and live the lives of our dreams if we will be productive.

I don't believe that anyone was ever given a goal, calling, or passion who didn't have the wherewithal to succeed;

therefore, success is a matter of maximizing our time and our effort.

All of us have 24 hours each day, and how we invest these hours will determine our success and our influence. Productivity is nothing more than getting the most out of every hour of every day. Productivity is like using a magnifying glass to focus the sun's rays. It can take something that is commonplace and turn it into a powerful force of energy.

Several years ago, I wrote a book entitled *The Art of Productivity* designed to help people get from where they are to where they want to be. I combined my efforts with the two most productive people I knew.

Steve Forbes wrote the foreword to *The Art of Productivity* and, along with Coach John Wooden, provided much of the wisdom and experience that made the book possible. We agreed that productivity must be broken down into its three components: motivation, communication, and implementation.

Without motivation, nothing that we would call success or productivity is even possible. People are motivated by recognition, money, inclusion, significance, legacy, and many other factors. As Coach Wooden said, "Some of my players were motivated by a gentle pat on the back; others needed to be patted a little lower and a lot harder."

If productivity begins with motivation, it certainly culminates with implementation. We live in a world that when it's all said and done, there's a great deal said and very little done. Productive people implement in a variety of methods. Some people multitask while others work in a linear fashion from one step to the next. Some people work as part of an ongoing team while others need to work in isolation and then bring their contribution to the team.

It is important that we find out what motivates everyone around us and how they best implement as we move toward our mutual goals. The bridge between motivation and implementation is communication. If, indeed, no one is an island, the bridge from our island to the rest of the world is our ability to communicate with others and have them communicate with us.

Just as we determined that people are motivated by different factors and implement in different ways, in researching *The Art of Productivity*, we came to understand that everyone in your personal and professional life will communicate in different ways. Coach Wooden drew on his decades of experience with basketball players to explain that some players need to see a play drawn up on the board while you can just tell other players what to do, and still other players need to walk through the play on the basketball floor.

The people you communicate with on a daily basis communicate best in a variety of ways. Some people need it in writing, others need to repeat it back to you, and still others need to walk through the concept you are discussing. A "one-size-fits-all" approach to communication will leave many people frustrated, and much of the detail you are trying to communicate will be lost.

If you or anyone with whom you live or work would like to determine and be able to share the methods of motivation, communication, and implementation that are the most productive for each individual, you can take my Productivity Assessment and get a free Productivity Profile by simply going to www.UltimateProductivity.com and using the access code 586404. The profile may seem simplistic to you or some of the people around you if you are an effective communicator; however, we have shared the Productivity Profile with top executives in Fortune 500 companies, military and political leaders, entrepreneurs, and many others, and they have all found hidden elements that can help them improve and will help you, your loved ones, and colleagues.

Productivity, success, and influence are a matter of doing what our role models do, so we can be our version of who they are and have the things that they have. Unfortunately, we live in a microwave culture, and success is often a crockpot process. It takes time to succeed and be influential. There are no shortcuts. You may be tempted to want to have what successful people have without being willing to do what they do or be who they are. Trying to have the trappings of wealth without earning them is a sure way to be poor. Debt is not your friend, and you can never borrow your way to influence.

Several years ago, there was a survey done of Fortune 500 executives. The researchers wanted to determine what elements and habits of these top executives' daily lives were most common. The survey explored their family status, political and religious beliefs, their health and exercise routines, and every other imaginable aspect of their lives. It was determined that the single factor that more of these top performers had in common than any other was the fact that they were avid readers. Not all readers are leaders, but all leaders are readers.

As you are reading this book that I have coauthored, I'm embarrassed to admit as you read these words on the page that when I had my eyesight and could read as you are doing now, I don't know that I ever read a whole book cover to cover. Reading was something I did just enough of to get through school but couldn't imagine reading beyond the classroom environment.

After losing my sight, I discovered audiobooks and high-speed listening. Today, I can listen to audiobooks at hundreds of words per minute, making it possible for me to read an entire book every day. There hasn't been a day in the last 30 years I haven't averaged reading more than one book.

Although I have met and worked with some of the most influential people of the last 30 years, the books I have read have influenced me even more than the people I've encountered. When you meet an individual you are considering for your dream team, you will invariably discuss their background, experience, and daily routines, but be sure to ask them about the most influential books they have read and the titles they are currently reading.

In much the same way books can influence us, movies and television can create lasting images that change our behavior, our performance, and our success.

I would encourage you to watch television and select movies much as our grandparents did. Today, people have a tendency to turn on the television and simply surf channels until they lose themselves in the midst of some program. This is not a good way to control our external influences.

Our grandparents consulted a TV guide and then selected the programs they wanted to watch throughout the week. While printed TV guides don't exist anymore, there are a number of apps and online services that can help you refine, control, and schedule the television and movies you are going to allow to influence you.

Success in any area of our lives will begin to make us influential, but we should never assume we are influencing others in the way we want to. We must control our influence and monitor it, or we will find that we are influencing people around us in ways we did not intend.

I have logged over two million miles flying with American Airlines. While I fly on most of the major carriers, American has the most convenient connections through my hometown. Someone told me that my business flights throughout the years are the equivalent of flying almost 100 times around the earth.

I remember arriving at the airport for a very early morning flight. I immediately noticed that the counter personnel and gate attendants were energetic and seemed to be in great moods. The airline employees were scurrying about politely and professionally, taking care of everything in an exemplary fashion. If you travel a lot, you know this is not always the case.

As a blind person myself and a first-class passenger, my assistant and I are generally the first two people on the plane. On this particular day when we boarded, there was one gentleman already seated across the aisle from us. I was curious as to who had gotten on the plane before me, so I stuck out my hand and introduced myself.

The gentleman shook my hand warmly and declared, "It's nice to meet you. I'm Robert Crandall."

I instantly realized that I was sitting across the aisle from the president of American Airlines, and I suddenly understood why the airline employees were on their best behavior.

After we took off, the outstanding employee performance continued throughout the meal and beverage service. Several of the flight attendants were grouped around Mr. Crandall in an effort to talk with him or provide the best service possible.

He asked several of the flight attendants their feelings about the new American Airlines incentive program he had apparently recently implemented. They gushed forth with praise and appreciation for Mr. Crandall and his plan.

Later in the flight, I got up to stretch my legs and walked a few steps forward to use the restroom. I stood there a moment waiting for another passenger to emerge from the restroom, so I was standing adjacent to the galley where the flight attendants do much of their work.

One flight attendant exclaimed, "Can you believe he thinks that incentive plan is motivating?"

Another flight attendant chimed in, "It's the most demotivating, demoralizing thing I've ever heard of."

A third flight attendant agreed, and they continued to discuss what they felt were the obvious shortcomings of Mr. Crandall's incentive plan.

When I returned to my seat across the aisle from Mr. Crandall, I realized that although he obviously had great influence within American Airlines, I actually knew more about how his new program was influencing his employees than he did.

Great influence is not the equivalent of effective influence in all cases. People often review their website or social media numbers to see how many people are accessing their information. Just because a lot of people are aware of you doesn't mean they are being influenced in the way you want them to be. Fame does not equal fortune, and popularity does not equal influence.

Lance Armstrong and Richard Nixon were both as well-known after their downfalls as they were before. They did not lose their celebrity status. They merely lost their positive influence.

If you are going to strive for success, build your influence, and create a lasting legacy. It is critical that you make sure you are on course and creating the influence that you intend.

CHAPTER TEN

THE INFLUENCE OF CONFLICT RESOLUTION IN PERSONAL AND PROFESSIONAL LIFE

RAY H. HULL, PhD

One of the most difficult challenges that we face in our personal and professional lives involves conflict resolution. Conflict resolution involves more creativity, more flexibility, and more resilience than any other form of human communication. But it is a form of communication in which every person who ventures forth into a personal relationship or profession of any kind must participate, at some time or another.

The resolution of conflict is required when people differ in their goals or their apparent needs and the means by which they attempt to achieve them. Their goals may be at cross-purposes with ours. The ability to resolve the conflict is one means of achieving resolution and cooperation.

A DELICATE FORM OF COMMUNICATION

Conflict resolution involves a delicate form of communication. It involves at least two people who may have differing opinions on how to achieve a goal, or differing opinions on how to achieve their own or their organization's needs. It does not involve coercion since coercion involves some form of threat either to the person or to their sense of self-esteem. Conflict resolution is not something that one person does *to* another person, but rather something that is done *with* another person.

What Is Involved in This Activity?

The following will give the reader ideas on how to constructively engage in the resolution of conflict through interpersonal communication, and how to resolve potential conflicts through indirect, and sometimes direct, interaction with those involved. None of these require a great deal of effort, but sometimes they DO require us to use the greatest amount of poise, charm, and patience that we can muster!

RESOLVING CONFLICT IN DAILY INTERACTIONS WITH OTHERS

1. In any situation that requires a positive resolution, there are things that we can do to resolve a potentially difficult encounter with a client or customer. There are some tips that have been found to defuse those encounters that require a positive resolution and a successful conclusion:

   - Shoot for a suitable resolution. Or rather, the goal should be to reach a *positive* solution. Compromise and a willingness to give a little, or as much as is possible, is the key.

   - Express your feelings, but perhaps not in great detail. Keeping them bottled up may result in an explosion of emotion that you will regret later.

- Communicate clearly and openly. Do not expect those with whom you are communicating to "read your mind."

- If an argument seems imminent, never— never take a cheap shot, no matter how easy it would be at the moment! No hitting below the belt, and absolutely no ridiculing! Don't say anything for which you must later give an apology!

- Don't make a big deal about a trivial issue. If you do, you need to consider why, and then ask yourself, "What am I really after?"

- And remember, timing is everything. Discuss a problem or a possible resolution to a problem at a time when your client or employee is emotionally ready for the discussion, which is definitely not just before lunch or on Friday afternoon after 5:00 pm!

- At some point, everyone fights dirty or may say things that they regret later. The best advice is to forgive, forget, and get over it. Be sure and give honest and sincere appreciation for the other person's expressed concerns or opinions.

- It is best to talk in terms of what the other person wants or needs and help her or him achieve it to the degree possible—

within reason—including those needs
that are non-monetary. In other words, we
must work diligently to see things from
the other person's point of view and work
with the person to resolve the concern in
the most equitable manner possible.

- Think—If this was my best friend or one
of my relatives, how would I resolve the
issue?

2. In resolving a potentially explosive confrontation with a staff member or client, here are
some suggestions for defusing it before it becomes a situation that is difficult to control.

What do you say?

- Your first inclination may be to say something to her that might be perceived as
an argument. But have you ever won an
argument? Be honest. Have you ever won
an argument? We may have thought we
won, but it is generally that the other
person simply gives up and says or thinks
something like, "Oh well..." or "I give
up...".

- In other words, the only way to get the
best of an argument is to avoid it. In the
meantime, try your best to make the other
person feel important, wanted, or needed,
but do it sincerely.

- So, what could emerge as a misunderstanding is never concluded successfully with an argument, but rather with tact, diplomacy, and a sincere desire to see the other person's point of view.

- It is frequently best to simply become a good listener. If we ask the person to expand on what she or he just said, and person explodes into a tirade as to the reasons for saying what she or he said, listening quietly is probably the best activity we can engage in at that moment. By allowing the person to vent, she or he may arrive at a solution on their own as we listen quietly or as we nudge the person in a positive direction.

- If another person seems to be intent on "rubbing you the wrong way," and your first instinct is to retaliate verbally, always distrust your first instinctive reaction to the situation. Pause, listen, and think first. Don't say something that you will later regret. It's much better avoid a confrontation than to have to apologize later.

- More than anything else, it is critically important that we control our temper!

- Always work diligently to see things from the other person's point of view. Failure in communication is almost assured if we consider situations or needs from our own standpoint.

- In resolving a conflict, look first for areas of agreement. Then, address the issues that are found on the other side of that coin.

- Always be honest, but not brutally honest! We are not involved in the discussion to offend, but to problem-solve.

- Importantly, we must control our initial instinct to give negative responses to something a person has just said.

WHAT CAN I DO TO BECOME A BETTER PROBLEM SOLVER?

In order to be an effective problem solver, we must develop insights that will help us to become a catalyst that will bring an atmosphere of calm to a situation. We must have the ability to analyze situations and become a calming and positive problem solver who can assist others in resolving issues in constructive ways. The insights that may evolve out of such interactions can become positive and constructive.

Since we all desire to develop that special ability to defuse otherwise potentially volatile situations, perhaps these suggestions will help:

- Remember, as I have learned the hard way, people like good listeners better than good talkers.

- So, one of the best ways to resolve potential difficulties is to be a good listener. The other person may resolve the potential problem on her or his own by talking it out while you listen quietly.

- If you see an argument on the horizon, become a good listener instead. Let the other person vent while you listen carefully. In other words, when people are speaking loudly, it is best for us to simply listen quietly.

- If nothing is resolved, as I said earlier, it is best to talk in terms of what the other person wants or needs. For example, let's say that a customer wants to return an item that he previously purchased from you. To avoid any type of confrontation or hard feelings with a customer, it is generally best to say something like, "I will be happy to return your money. And, if we can serve you again in the future, be sure and come back to see us. It has been good working with you." At that, you simply return the customer's money. You can be assured that he will return in the future, and he will do business with the assurance that he will be well treated. He has been treated with kindness and respect and will probably refer other customers to you. Your simple gesture of goodwill will go a long way toward increasing business at your establishment!

WHEN RESOLVING A POTENTIAL CONFLICT, HOW CAN I ADMIT THAT I MAY BE WRONG?

There are occasions in our professional life when we have studied an issue carefully and are sure that our decision regarding a potential resolution to that issue is solid and workable. In discussing the issue in a staff meeting, you present the solution that you are sure is the best and most productive one. Further, you provide the rationale and a process for implementing the resolution. After a moment of silence, a fellow staff member provides an alternative solution that, as you think about it, makes absolute sense and appears to be a much more workable method for resolving the problem. How do you admit that the solution that she proposed appears to be a much better one and still save face in the eyes of your fellow staff members?

Here are some ideas:

- Rather than holding rigidly to your first resolution to a problem, it is important to remember that you will never get into trouble by admitting that the resolution that you thought was foolproof and the best avenue to resolving the problem may not be the best one. It can even improve your standing among your staff members when you admit that your colleague's idea seems to be a better one and congratulate her or him for the great idea!

- Remember, in many instances, it is not the fear of being right or wrong that creates confrontations between two people, but rather the threat to the other person's self-esteem. It is natural for us to want to be right, and it takes a high level of maturity to admit that we may be wrong or need further advice or evidence.

- If a fellow staff member presents their idea as a resolution to an issue confronting your organization, and the other members unanimously vote it down as a bad idea, we must do whatever is possible to help the other person save face. No matter how wrong we might think the other person is, we only destroy ego and potentially good interpersonal relationships by embarrassing the other person. Hurting someone's dignity does nothing to resolve issues or solve problems. And dignity is essential to self-esteem.

Here is a situation to think about: You are holding a staff meeting to discuss business expenses, purchases, and equipment needs for the coming year. The discussion becomes somewhat heated. What do you do?

- Have you ever had a salesperson say during a discussion about purchasing a car, "Let's work for win-win!"? You could discuss adding air conditioning or a better grade stereo system. But, when you think about it, win-win never really is. There is no such thing. Win-win is really give and take. You have to determine what you are willing to give up in order to make the other person feel that they have "won" at least to some degree.

- In other words, it is important to be creative! Effective conflict resolution or problem solving involves creative thinking—the development of creative ideas.

- However, the greatest enemy to creativity is criticism. By all means, don't criticize when another person has come up with what he or she thinks is a good idea! Saying "Thank you" and giving sincere appreciation for effort can make creativity blossom, while criticism can destroy it. An atmosphere of appreciation is fertile ground for the creation of good ideas and successful communication.

- And, importantly, in working with business associates (and in raising children), demand is an ugly word. It makes rational adults (and children) react irrationally. We can, however, have points that are necessarily, and for important reasons, non-negotiable.

- If you know you are correct in regard to a certain point of contention because you have done your research and have data to prove a point, state your findings without fanfare. If

you present your findings quietly, people will
be more apt to accept what you have to say.

- If you find that the situation has become one
that you were not expecting, and you are not
sure what you are to do, don't try to create a
new personality in an attempt to fit the situation. That usually doesn't work because the
new personality isn't really *you*. You should
simply control your own personality to your
best advantage.

CONFLICT CAN BE AN OPPORTUNITY FOR GROWTH

Here's another situation to think about:

You have worked with the same group of people for a
number of years, and you all know each other well. Still, in
some staff meetings, conflict arises, and the conflict seems
to consistently arise from one member of your staff—one of
the best and most trusted members of your team.

What do you do?

- No matter how close we are to those with
whom we work and play, we cannot be
expected to be in agreement on all issues all
the time. If we learn to work together positively in resolving conflict, then we tend to
grow, and our relationships likewise tend to
grow and strengthen as a result. If we understand the nature of conflict and the reasons
for it, we can:

a. Develop the capacity to recognize and respond to things that matter to the other person.

b. Develop calm, non-defensive, and respectful reactions to conflict.

c. Develop a readiness to forgive and forget and to move past the conflict without holding resentment and anger.

d. Develop the ability to seek compromise and avoid holding grudges.

e. Establish your belief that facing conflict directly is the best avenue for both sides.[18]

f. Know when to let something go. If we can't come to an agreement, then we can simply agree to disagree. Remember, it takes two people to keep an argument going. If a conflict is going nowhere, it is appropriate to disengage and move on. But, in moving on, we can still shake hands and smile. We can still love and appreciate the other person, even though we don't agree!

CHAPTER ELEVEN

THE LEGACY OF INFLUENCE

The most significant legacy we will leave behind is not our money. It is our influence.
—JIM STOVALL

O ur legacy of influence can be either good or bad and may not be apparent until long after we're gone. Only 11 people attended Karl Marx's funeral in 1883, but by the middle of the next century, more than half the people on earth were living under the influence of the political and governmental system he had created.

Vincent van Gogh never sold a painting during his life, but in the last 70 days prior to his death by suicide, he created over 100 masterpieces. His legacy remains a creative output that has never been equaled in the art world.

Our lasting influence may be a lifetime of service or a simple phrase. Who could ever forget immortal, influential words such as "I have a dream," "A day which shall live in infamy," or "Do you believe in miracles?"

Whether you are a civil rights leader, the president of the United States, or a broadcaster covering the Olympics, a simple phrase can define your life and create a legacy of influence. Sometimes your legacy of influence can even be nonverbal.

My father worked for over 57 years for one nonprofit organization. At the height of his career, he managed hundreds of clerical and administrative employees. I remember running into one of his former workers in a restaurant. She shared with me her lasting memory of my father and the influence that he had on her.

Apparently, they were having difficulties with a number of employees arriving late to the office. According to his former colleague, my father didn't call a meeting, send out a memo, or even talk to the workers. He simply observed that all employees parked in a lot down a long hill from the office. There was a sidewalk that connected the parking lot to a set of stairs that led up to a large veranda area outside the entrance to the building. This veranda area commanded a sweeping view of the hillside and the entire parking lot.

My father dealt with the tardiness challenge by simply drinking his morning coffee standing on the veranda at the top of the stairs where he greeted all of his arriving colleagues. Nothing ever had to be said, nor was anyone threatened or reprimanded, but the tardiness problem was resolved.

For several decades, there has been a trend in the corporate world of every organization having a mission statement that reflects their identity and goals. As important as it may be for organizations to have a mission statement that is truly meaningful to all concerned, it is even more important that you and I have a personal mission statement that defines our personal and professional journey toward our own definition of success.

I have had a personal mission statement of this kind for several years. I would like to tell you that I created it by myself, but in reality, my personal mission statement was given to me secondhand from my grandmother.

My grandmother played a vital role at several critical points in my life. When I was very young, I had a sister who was a couple of years older than me. She became very ill with what was later diagnosed as a form of leukemia. Due to her illness and my parents' subsequent travels taking her from hospital to hospital and specialist to specialist across the country, I spent a lot of time with my grandparents as a very young child.

Some of my earliest memories are of my grandparents and learning valuable lessons from people who had gone through a depression, a world war, and the building of what we know as the modern world. Tom Brokaw labeled these individuals collectively as The Greatest Generation. While I agree with Mr. Brokaw's assessment, I don't believe that generation was created with any more greatness than we are. They simply were confronted with circumstances that required great people.

Several years later as a teenager, I was diagnosed with a very serious eye disease that would eventually rob me of my sight. In that time of adjustment from being fully sighted to partially sighted and then moving into blindness, I remember my grandmother being a tremendous support and encouragement. Through her words and deeds, she taught me the difference between sight and vision.

I learned that sight is the ability to see the world around you by capturing images through your eyes into your mind. Vision is the ability to capture the world around you in your mind as it should be and make it a reality. Both sight and vision are valuable commodities, but as a person who has lived with and without both, given the choice I would prefer vision to sight.

In my twenties, I spent some time as a Wall Street investment broker and then, as a totally blind person, launched a company called the Narrative Television Network which makes movies, television, and educational programming accessible to 13 million blind and visually impaired Americans and many millions more around the world. Through that process of building a successful company and being recognized at the White House as the Entrepreneur of the Year and then recognized by the U.S. Chamber of Commerce as the Businessperson of the Year, I began receiving invitations to speak at corporate and arena events across the country.

Somehow, as happens to all of us, years passed without my noticing, and my grandmother became quite elderly and was approaching the end of her life. Arrangements were made so she could spend most of her last months, weeks, and days in her own home surrounded by the things and the people that she loved and that made her most comfortable.

I made quite a few trips during this period to her home in another state. On what turned out to be my last visit, I arrived when she was already asleep for the night. Her nurse was sitting outside her room and greeted me. I told her I wished I could have arrived earlier in the day, but a business commitment had delayed me. The nurse told me that my grandmother was aware of that and was very proud of the work I did.

This really surprised me as I had never known that my grandmother really understood what I did for a living. When you're the first entrepreneur in your family, it's a little hard for the elder generations to grasp the concept.

The nurse laughed softly, took my hand, and quietly led me through the doorway into my grandmother's room. The nurse whispered, "Beside her bed there is a picture of you holding the Emmy Award you received. Every person that comes into this house is told the same explanation from your grandmother. She points to that picture and tells them, · 'This is my grandson. He does two things. He helps blind people see television, and he travels around the world, telling people they can have good things in their lives.'"

As influential as that was at that time, the true import of it is still dawning upon me many years later. I didn't realize it at the time, and I'm quite certain my grandmother never heard of a personal mission statement, but without realizing it, through a private duty night nurse, my grandmother had given me my personal mission statement.

Helping to identify who you are and what you do may be the greatest legacy of influence. If your influence is going to expand beyond your own efforts and potentially extend beyond your life, you've got to consider protocol and systems.

Micah White was the leader of the Occupy Wall Street protest movement and previously participated in several similar demonstrations. Whether you agree or disagree with Mr. White's sentiments, you would at least have to recognize that his efforts garnered worldwide attention, but according to Micah White's book, *The End of Protest*, he felt he and his followers failed to have a lasting influence.

If you have hundreds, thousands, or even hundreds of thousands of people marching and carrying signs, you may get on the nightly news, but you may also have failed to have

a legacy of influence. Mr. White explained that his dem-
onstrators wanted to protest in front of the TV cameras but
didn't want to go up on Capitol Hill to lobby members of
Congress and senators.

There is a legal system in place, and if you want your
protests to be anything more than angry complaints, you
need to put your influence to work within the system. For
better or for worse, there are bureaucracies, organizational
structures, and systems that exist. They can provide leverage
for your influence if you work within them but can create
barriers to your influence if you work outside of them.

I have a good friend who is a fellow author named Chuck
Sasser. Chuck served as a war correspondent and special
forces leader in the military, and then had a distinguished
career as a homicide detective.

I was invited to a reunion which included a number of
former soldiers Chuck had served with in the special forces.
I was struck by the fact that as each of them was leaving at
the end of the evening, they warmly embraced and hugged
one another. Some of them had seen one another the previous day, but the hugs and embraces were repeated every time
they were together.

I asked Chuck the rationale behind this behavior, and he
explained, "When you've been in some of the life-and-death
situations we've been in, you realize that every goodbye
could be the last one."

I believe that sentiment is not only valid for special
forces soldiers but the rest of us as well. If we realize that
every encounter we have with everyone else may be our

last one, we understand that our legacy may be made up of one small comment, incident, or action. If we live our lives as if each day might be our final one, and every encounter might be the last one, we will live our lives better and much more carefully.

My late, great friend, colleague, and mentor, the legendary Coach John Wooden, was fond of telling his players and people around the world, including me, that before you undertake any activity, task, or encounter with another person, you should ask yourself one simple question: "What would I do now if I were amazing?"

That simple question has guided me in my best moments, and invariably, looking back on some of my worst moments, I discover that I have avoided answering that influential question or even asking it in the first place. You've heard it said that anything worth doing is worth doing right, but if you want to go to the next level and have a legacy of influence, ask yourself, "What would I do now if I were amazing?"

Each time I complete a TV program, movie, newspaper column, speech, or a book, including the one you're reading now, I try to imagine someone encountering my work 100 years from now in their grandmother's dusty attic. My fervent hope is that my efforts will have had influence, and my work will not simply be an antique or curiosity but, instead, will remain an enduring influence now and into the future.

CHAPTER TWELVE

THE ART AND INFLUENCE OF LEADERSHIP

RAY H. HULL, PhD

What makes an effective leader in the field of business? In fact, what constitutes an effective leader in any field? We all desire to be successful in our profession, but can we truly be successful without becoming someone others look up to?

Every one of us desires success in some form. If we don't desire to be successful, what else is there? We watch and observe those who are successful in their chosen occupation. We watch professional football players who are the successful ones—the leaders in their field—who have practiced until their skills are honed. We watch professional golfers—the ones who win the coveted green jacket. We watch professional musicians who have made it in the world of professional jazz or classical music. We observe entrepreneurs who become multimillionaires—those who have failed once or twice and then rebounded. You know who they are—the Bill Gates and Steve Jobs of the computer world, for example. They have been described as leaders in their field.

How about the field in which you work? Who are the leaders? How many can you name? Is it you or someone else who is currently, or was in the past, considered to be a leader?

WHAT IS A LEADER? WHAT ARE THE CHARACTERISTICS OF THOSE WHO ARE CONSIDERED TO BE LEADERS?

In searching through the literature on the topic of "leadership," I have found that there are characteristics that consistently emerge in those who are considered to be leaders in their field, including yours and mine:

1. First of all, leadership isn't about the position you hold. Many people have been assigned leadership positions when they have no reason to be there. I've heard people say, "I know a leader when I see one." But then they can't describe what a leader is. Well, if you can't describe leadership, will you ever be one?

2. If you want to make an impact on your world, to become a leader in whatever your world may be, learning what constitutes becoming a leader is critical to achieving that level of success. Among others, those characteristics include:

   a. Being respectful.

   b. Being intuitive.

   c. Being an effective and open communicator.

   d. Being a good listener.

   e. Being respectful of those with whom you work.

   f. Being honest.

   g. Being an innovator.

   h. Being one who will sacrifice time and effort to support those with whom one works.

   i. Giving honest praise and compliments to your associates and employees.

    j. Being interested in serving others—rather than yourself.

    k. Being a creative problem solver.

    l. Being one who inspires coworkers by your example.

3. Leaders take calculated risks but are by no means risky.

    a. Rather, they push themselves hard for the good of the organization they serve.

    b. They listen willingly.

    c. They tell the truth.

    d. They go out of their way to make the organization a fun place to work.

    e. Most of all, they communicate in an empathetic manner. It's called "human leadership."

    f. They believe that people are to be valued.

Other traits of great leaders include the following, paraphrasing from Brian Tracy's "The 7 Best Leadership Qualities":[19]

1. Great leaders have a clear, exciting idea of where they are going and what they desire to accomplish.

2. They demonstrate courage. That means that every decisive action they take is made with no assurance of success, but they take action that

they believe is for the good of the organization anyway.

3. They possess integrity which means truthfulness to all people and in every situation.

4. They demonstrate humility. Great leaders are strong and decisive but also humble. They do not boast of their accomplishments.

5. Great leaders are willing to admit when they could be wrong, that they are not perfect in all endeavors.

6. Great leaders have the ability to look ahead, to anticipate where their organization should be headed, and should be able to anticipate what it will take to ensure that their organization will be ahead of the competition.

According to Hasan, leadership is defined by a number of qualities that everyone should aspire to attain.[20] He includes the following:

1. *They model honesty and integrity*

He writes that those are two ingredients that make a good leader.

How can one who aspires to be a good leader expect their associates or employees to be honest and exhibit integrity if they do not exhibit that quality themselves?

2. They inspire others

Being a great leader means that the leader inspires others by setting a good example. When the going gets rough, according to Hasan, the leader's associates or employees look up to her or him to see how the leader reacts to the situation. If the leader handles it well, they will tend to follow suit.

3. They are committed and possess passion

Commitment and passion are two important qualities of a great leader. If a great leader wants those with whom they associate on a daily basis to give their all to the tasks at hand, then the leader must demonstrate that they are committed and passionate about the goal.

4. They must be a good communicator

Effective communication is essential to leadership. If one is not an effective communicator, they will never be a great leader. A great leader must have the ability to communicate well and to motivate those with whom they associate in their organization or business through effective communication. Words have power, and great leaders use them to motivate others. I will speak about that characteristic a little later in this chapter.

5. They must exhibit creativity and innovation

Great leaders think out of the box. A great leader must be both creative and innovative. Great leaders have great ideas and turn them into reality when it is possible.

6. *They demonstrate empathy*

I can think of individuals in our world today who aspire to be great leaders but rather become dictators. They fail to communicate well with those for whom they are responsible. They lose connection with them.

They do not demonstrate empathy or a caring nature in their interactions with those in their organization or workplace. And that can be the downfall of one who might otherwise have become a great leader.

As I said above:

THOSE WHO ASPIRE TO BE GREAT LEADERS MUST BE EXCELLENT COMMUNICATORS

The ability to communicate well is essential to good leadership. Earlier in this book, I said that with all else in our favor, we should do well in a position of leadership. I emphasized the word *should* in that sentence.

The reason? The reason is that there are many people who find themselves in leadership positions who do not do as well as they expected. They possess the qualities that comprise a good leader except for one—that is, the ability to communicate well with those for whom they are responsible, the ability to impress audiences with their manner of speaking, their ability to inspire those who he or she desires to impress that would encourage their business enterprise to flourish. In other words, the ability to communicate effectively is essential to anyone who aspires to be recognized as a leader.

So, what are some indicators of those who communicate well? Here are 16 suggestions as found earlier in this book:

- No matter how bad the day, don't place it on your clients or associates by telling them about it.

- Be appropriate in all behaviors—no off-color jokes or remarks no matter how innocent they seem to you.

- Be pleasant, be a genuinely good person, be empathetic, and be nice.

- Be a good ambassador to your profession.

- Remember this rule—We are here to serve, not to judge.

- Be flexible. Be a creative problem solver.

- Affirm your commitment to serving people, and emphasize how much you enjoy the opportunity.

- Listen carefully and quietly to what the other person is saying to you, no matter how urgently you want them to know that you already have the solution to their problem. In other words, don't interrupt!

- When listening to another person, never look at your watch!

- Be empathetic, but never respond by saying, "I know just how you feel," unless you have clearly experienced what the other person is expressing.

- Remember to speak at a slightly slower rate than your usual speed of speech. You will be much more easily understood. When you slow your rate of speech, a natural result is that you will articulate with greater clarity.

- Maintain good eye contact, but do not stare at the person you are speaking with. For best eye contact, concentrate on the speaker's nose. Do not look into their eyes. That level of intimacy is not appropriate unless you intend to ask the person to marry you!

OTHER CHARACTERISTICS OF GREAT LEADERS

1. *Maturity*

According to Hasan, contrary to popular belief, age is not a measure of maturity. Maturity involves being courteous, communicating like an adult, not a teenager. An indicator of maturity is confidence and the ability to follow through with difficult tasks without excuses.

2. *Lead by Example*

Leaders lead by example. Actions speak louder than words, so it is said, and those who associate with one who aspires to be a leader will notice if she or he is dedicated and setting a positive example for others in the organization.

3. Speaking Skills

One who aspires to be a leader should not have difficulty speaking in front of an audience—large or small. Getting one's message across to a group of associates or a large audience is critically important to the art of leadership.

4. Being Bold

Those who are great leaders do not appear fearful. They take hold of difficult issues, they look at all sides of those issues, they consult with others they trust, and based on all sides of issues, they make decisions that make sense in light of all the information that is available to them. They are willing to take hold of issues despite the risks.

5. Possess Compassion

Compassion is essential to great leadership. Those with whom the leader works and otherwise associates must know that their leader is compassionate and cares about them and about others. They know that their leader will do nothing to harm them or their feelings. They know that the leader truly cares about them and demonstrates it.

6. Not Afraid to Delegate Responsibility

Those who are insecure in their position or their ability to work with others do not make good leaders. Great leaders do not hesitate to delegate responsibility to others in their organization when such delegation is appropriate and reasonable. They are comfortable in their position and the responsibilities that they have, and likewise feel comfortable requesting that others accept some responsibility for duties within the organization.

I was reading a book the other day entitled *The Articulate Executive*, authored by Toogood. In it, he discusses the characteristics of a leader. He states, for example:

- That Lee Iacocca pulled Chrysler back from near ashes. He had it.

- That John Sculley built Apple into a world power that challenged IBM. He had it.

- That John Welch made General Electric the model of the early 21st-century corporation. He had it.

- That Norman Schwarzkopf leaped out of nowhere to humble Saddam Hussein in Desert Storm and then dazzled the world with press briefings that brought a new element of humanity, wisdom, and restraint to the public perception of war. He had it.[21]

Toogood states that all four brought more than just competence to their jobs, they exemplified what is embedded in the word "leadership." They exemplified (1) competence; (2) clarity, since they were able to see beyond their "job"; (3) the belief that change can be good; (4) the insight of where they ought to be headed; and (5) communication, since they must be able to communicate effectively, explain, share, translate clearly and with the ability to help the doubters to believe, be a teacher, and then become a leader. Toogood states, and the author of this chapter truly believes, that, "The only way you can ever be a leader is to learn to speak effectively," and, may I add, with clarity![22] Lee Iacocca exemplified that quality. He raised Chrysler from rubble to one of the top automobile manufacturers in the U.S., and he did it by his ability to persuade and inspire. That, in and of itself, exemplifies leadership.

I like another series of statements by Toogood who says, "The role of management is changing fast. Managers, today, are expected to lead (be a leader). You can't hide in your office anymore and hope that all will go well, that the business or enterprise will somehow run itself. Now you've got to roll up your sleeves, get out of the corner office and executive suite, and down on the floor. You've got to show *leadership*. You've got to become a coach and a facilitator. You've got to encourage risk taking. You've got to be seen and heard. You've got to inspire others to share your vision."[23]

In other words, you have to become a leader. A leader cannot simply delegate authority and sit in his or her office and wait for calamity to occur. That's not the way the world of business or any organization works nowadays.

It is interesting that in every treatise on the topic of leadership that I have read, the necessity of effective communication is inevitably present. However, as I said earlier in this book in the chapter on "communication," it is interesting that programs that prepare professionals in the vast majority of fields of service, including medicine, education, dentistry, cosmetology, carpentry, plumbing, landscaping, public administration, educational administration, and the majority of others, do not offer formal preparation in this critically important aspect of their profession.

As I said, this is a sad state for any profession since communication plays a vitally important role in attracting and maintaining one's clientele and advancing in one's profession or into positions of leadership.

One of the comments that I frequently hear as I advise others about effective communication is, "I meet with my staff once a month to go over sales figures, ideas on how we can increase business contacts, and try to build everyone on our staff of fifty employees up with compliments on their commitment to the company and how well they can do if they set their minds to their tasks. But then everything seems to go right back to the way it was before the meeting! What am I doing wrong?"

My response is, "First of all, it is great that you are meeting with your staff on a regular basis. That is positive and a good start. But do you ever go to their offices to sit down and talk? Do you ask questions? Do you ask if they have any concerns or ideas on how to increase productivity of your company? In other words, do you share ideas and opinions and ask the opinions of your staff? Do you go to the floor where everyone is working, then give them a pep talk? Do you go to the floor and share in their workload to see what really goes on in the daily lives of your employees? In other words, are you functioning as a leader?"

As I said earlier in this book, when I am working with those who find themselves in responsible positions within business and industry, I stress to them that clear and effective communication is not only essential to good leadership, but also an essential ingredient within leadership that influences others in positive ways, the influence that motivates them to move in the directions that the leader has intended. In other words, the person to whom the leader of the organization or business is providing direction understands what was said, is motivated, and in turn begins to move in the direction that the leader intended in the first place.

The leader then discovers probably the most important ingredient for both effective leadership and the ability to be a positive influence on the lives of those with whom they work. By using clear and effective communication, they find that employees hear and, most importantly, understand what the leader is saying to them.

Chen, who I referred to earlier in this book, feels that there is a need to explore the relationship between communication within complex organizations and the performance of workers, since communication is the integrating component between organizational units and the functions within the total organization. He feels that communication is the activity that links people together and creates relationships within organizations. He says that communication is the glue that binds people together within an organization, and leaders are the key to good communication.[24]

That is one good reason to avoid the use of computers for purposes of interoffice communication as much as possible. Face-to-face communication is a positive link that good leaders use. Using computers as a major form of interoffice communication results in faceless interactions between members of staff and managers and their staff. It is a major reason for a lack of communication within companies, schools, universities, and other organizations where communication plays a major role in workers' ability to function effectively and efficiently.

A FINAL THOUGHT

One final thought: Distrust is a major cause of the downfall of some leaders. One reason why many so-called leaders are distrusted today is that they are seen as self-serving—primarily interested in themselves rather than others. To be an effective and respected leader, it is critical that we develop good habits in working with people—I mean all those one works with, all those who are served, not just one's inner circle. An effective leader is there for all of her or his people, is willing to sacrifice time and effort for the good of the company and the people who work there, and shows unbridled confidence in those she or he has employed.

That is leadership!

CHAPTER THIRTEEN

THE INFLUENTIAL CONCLUSION

When it's all said and done, there is too often a lot said and very little done.
—JIM STOVALL

My dear reader, whether you realize it or not, you have given me one of the greatest honors and compliments I receive within my professional life. You expended your time, money, and effort to read this book. My fervent hope is that you have enjoyed this book and learned something from it, but if that is all that happens in your life as a result of reading this book, I will feel as if I have not succeeded in having the influence that I want to have.

I have the privilege of regularly speaking to millions of people in corporate and arena events. Millions of my books have sold and have been released in dozens of languages around the world. My eight novels that have been turned into movies have influenced a countless number of people and groups, from public classrooms to corporate boardrooms and theatres around the world. My weekly columns are read by a myriad of people on four continents in hundreds of newspapers, magazines, and online publications each week. The Narrative Television Network is available in virtually every home in North America and millions more around the world.

Every time I have contact with an individual, whether it's in print, on a screen, or from the stage, I want to have a lasting influence that impacts their future. However I may engage or encounter my audience, I always leave them with a way to stay connected with me. You can reach me any time via Jim@JimStovall.com. Through my colleague, Dorothy Thompson, to whom I have dictated this book as well as all my others, I respond to every email sent to me.

While I appreciate finding out how much people may have enjoyed one of my books, columns, speeches, or movies, I am grateful when they share with me how the information has influenced them to change their lives.

This final section of the book is not the end of our encounter. It is just the beginning of what I hope will be a lasting influence on your life and career so you can, in turn, have a legacy of influence on everyone around you as well as throughout your life and beyond.

CORNERSTONES

BY JIM STOVALL

If I am to dream, let me dream magnificently.
Let me dream grand and lofty thoughts and ideals
That are worthy of me and my best efforts.
If I am to strive, let me strive mightily.
Let me spend myself and my very being
In a quest for that magnificent dream.
And, if I am to stumble, let me stumble but persevere.
Let me learn, grow, and expand myself
to join the battle renewed –
Another day and another day and another day.
If I am to win, as I must, let me do so
with honor, humility, and gratitude
For those people and things that

have made winning possible
And so very sweet.
For each of us has been given life
as an empty plot of ground
With four cornerstones.
These four cornerstones are the ability to dream,
The ability to strive,
The ability to stumble but persevere,
And the ability to win.
The common man sees his plot of ground as little more
Than a place to sit and ponder the
things that will never be.
But the uncommon man sees his
plot of ground as a castle,
A cathedral,
A place of learning and healing.
For the uncommon man understands
that in these four cornerstones
The Almighty has given us
anything—and everything.

ENDNOTES

ERFUL SOURCE OF INFLUENCE

1. NI Chen, "Internal/Employee Communication and Organizational Effectiveness," *Journal of Contemporary China* 17, no. 54 (2008): 167-189.

2   José R. Goris, "Effects of Satisfaction with Communication on the Relationship between Individual-Job Congruence and Job Performance/ Satisfaction," *Journal of Management Development* 26, no. 8 (2007): 737-752, and Roderick M. Kramer, "Trust and Distrust in Organizations: Emerging Perspectives, Enduring Questions," *Annual Review of Psychology* 50 (1999): 569-598.

3   Marcia Zidle, "Power is Not a Bad Word," Free Management Library, last modified 2017, http:// managementhelp.org/leading people/influencing-others .htm

4   "What is Interpersonal Communication?" Skills You Need, UK Web Archive, 2010, https://www. skillsyouneed.com/ips/interpersonal-communication .html

CHAPTER 4: THE POWER AND INFLUENCE OF IMAGE AND PUBLIC RELATIONS

5. "Professional Image," accessed October 15, 2017, https://swsu.ru/sbornik-statey/pdf/pro_image_ch01.pdf

6. Yasmin Anderson-Smith, "Expert Advice For Creating a Professional Image in the Workplace," ExpertBeacon, accessed October 31, 2017, https://expertbeacon.com/expert-advice-creating-professional-image-workplace/#.WwSS4VMvz-Z

7. American Association of Employment in Education, "What is Professional Image?" *Career Corner* (blog), *Education Week*, March 30, 2011, http://blogs.edweek.org/topschooljobs/careers/2011/03

8. Brett and Kate McKay, *The Art of Manliness: Classic Skills and Manners for the Modern Man* (Cincinnati, Ohio: HOW Books, 2009).

9. Sherie Campbell, *Loving Yourself: The Mastery of Being Your Own Person* (Bloomington, Indiana: AuthorHouse, 2012).

10. Rosabeth Moss Kanter, *The Change Masters* (New York: Simon & Schuster, 1983), 247.

11. Dale Carnegie, *How to Win Friends and Influence People* (New York: Pocket Books, 1936), 73.

12. Carnegie, *How to Win Friends and Influence People*, 99.

13. Jean Prather, "Civility and Respect in the Workplace," Rose-Hulman Institute of Technology, 2016, http://studylib.net/doc/11674096/civility-andamp%3B

ITY AND RESPECT IN THE WORKPLACE

14. L.M. Cortina et al., "Incivility in the Workplace: Incidence and Impact," *Journal of Occupational Health Psychology* 6, no. 1 (2001): 64-80.

15. S. Chris Edmonds, "Four Steps Proven To Cultivate Workplace Civility," *Forbes*, Forbes Coaches Council, April 14, 2017, https://www.forbes.com/sites/forbescoachescouncil/2017/04/14/four-steps-proven-to-cultivate-workplace-civility/#37f970ba37cf

CHAPTER 8: THE INFLUENCE OF LEARNING: LEARNING THAT INFLUENCES US THROUGHOUT OUR LIVES

The Art of Learning and Self-Development (Shippensburg, PA: Sound Wisdom, 2017).

17. Amy Soller, "Supporting Social Interaction in an Intelligent Collaborative Learning System," *International Journal of Artificial Intelligence in Education* 12 (2001): 40-62.

CHAPTER 10: THE INFLUENCE OF CONFLICT RESOLUTION IN PERSONAL AND PROFESSIONAL LIFE

18. Skills: Building the Skills That Can Turn Conflicts into Opportunities," *HelpGuide*, January 2018, https://www.helpguide.org/articles/relationships-communication/conflict-resolution-skills .htm

CHAPTER 12: THE ART AND INFLUENCE OF LEADERSHIP

19. Brian Tracy, "The Top 7 Leadership qualities and Attributes of Great Leaders," *Brian Tracy International*, 2017, https://www.briantracy.com/blog/leadership-success/the-seven-leadership-qualities-of-great-leaders-strategic-planning/

20. Sarmad Hasan, "Top 10 Leadership Qualities That Make Good Leaders," *Taskque* (blog), February 13, 2017, https://blog.taskque.com/characteristics-good-leaders/.

21. Granville N. Toogood, *The Articulate Executive: Learn to Look, Act, and Sound Like A Leader* (New York: McGraw-Hill, 1996), 9.

22 Toogood, 10.

23. Toogood, 13.

24. NI Chen, "Internal/Employee Communication and Organizational Effectiveness," *Journal of Contemporary China* 17, no. 54 (2008): 189.

FURTHER SUGGESTED READING

Bradbury, Andrew. *Successful Publication Skills*. Philadelphia, PA: Kogan Page, 2006.

Campbell, Rex. *Leadership: Getting it Done*, 2016, https://missouri.app.box.com/s/7hgspqvkybnooj9vvuzew42bg5colv6e/1/11053612080

Doward, Brian. "101 Leadership Skills, Traits, and Qualities—The Complete List." *Brian Doward* (blog), last accessed June 11, 2018, http://briandownard.com/leadership-skills-list/

Hickson, Mark, and Stacks, Don. *Nonverbal Communication: Studies and Applications*. Dubuque, IA: Wm C. Brown Communications, 2000.

Koegel, Timothy. *The Exceptional Presenter: A Proven Formula to Open up and Own the Room*. Austin, TX: Greenleaf Book Group, 2007.

Lieberman, David. *Make Peace with Anyone: Breakthrough Strategies to Quickly End Any Conflict, Feud, or Estrangement*. New York: St. Martin's Press, 2002.

Marshall, Lisa. *Small Talk: The Public Speaker's Guide to Success in Every Situation*. New York: St. Martin's Press, 2013.

Mckay, Dawn Rosenberg. "Why You Need Excellent Listening Skills." *The Balance Careers*. March 6, 2017. https://www.thebalancecareers.com/listening -skills-524853

Reardon, Kathleen. *Persuasion in Practice*. Newbury Park, CA: Sage, 1991.

Smith, Dennis and L. Keith Williamson. *Interpersonal Communication: Roles, Rules, Strategies, and Games.* Dubuque, IA: Wm C. Brown, 1985.

Williams, Scott. "Listening Effectively." 2002. http://www .wright.edu/~scott.williams/skills/listening.htm

Wilson, Gerald L., Alan Hantz, and Michael Hanna. *Interpersonal Growth through Communication*. Dubuque, IA: Wm C. Brown Publishers, 1990.

ABOUT JIM STOVALL

In spite of blindness, Jim Stovall has been a national Olympic weightlifting champion, a successful investment broker, the president of the Emmy Award-winning Narrative Television Network, and a highly sought-after author and platform speaker. He is the author of 40 books including the bestseller *The Ultimate Gift*, which is now a major motion picture from Twentieth Century Fox starring James Garner and Abigail Breslin. Five of his other novels have also been made into movies with two more in production.

Steve Forbes, president and CEO of *Forbes* magazine, says, "Jim Stovall is one of the most extraordinary men of our era."

For his work in making television accessible to our nation's 13 million blind and visually impaired people, the President's Committee on Equal Opportunity selected Jim Stovall as the Entrepreneur of the Year. Jim Stovall has been featured in *The Wall Street Journal*, *Forbes* magazine, *USA Today*, and has been seen on *Good Morning America*, *CNN*, and *CBS Evening News*. He was also chosen as the International Humanitarian of the Year, joining Jimmy Carter, Nancy Reagan, and Mother Teresa as recipients of this honor.

Jim Stovall can be reached at 918-627-1000 or Jim@JimStovall.com.

ABOUT RAY HULL, PHD

Ray Hull, PhD, was born and raised on a farm in central Kansas. He attended a rural, two-room school and was taught by a teacher by the name of Mrs. Hamilton. In that school, a single teacher taught students for four consecutive years in the same classroom. Mrs. Hamilton had a great influence on Ray. Her positive influence is reflected in two of the chapters in this book.

Ray was a severe stutterer from early childhood on into his adult years. His struggles to rid himself of that "plague to communication" as he called it, and his attempts to "cure" himself of the stuttering during his high school and college years propelled him into a world of successful public speaking and acting as a radio disk jockey, television announcer, and an award-winning actor and public speaker.

Dr. Hull is currently Professor of Communication Sciences and Disorders, Neuroscience in the College of Health Professions at Wichita State University. He was Chair of the Department of Communication Disorders at University of Northern Colorado for 12 years; held administrative posts within the graduate school, being responsible for graduate program review and evaluation; was the Director of Planning and Budget for the Office of the President for seven successful years at the University of Northern Colorado, responsible for the allocation of over $60 million in state-appropriated funds.

BACKGROUND

His background in the fields of communication disorders and the neuroscience of human communication began with his college degree in public speaking, drama, and radio/television broadcast, and then moved into graduate work in disorders of human communication, and then a doctorate in the neurosciences of human communication that involved a combined doctoral degree from the University of Colorado School of Medicine and the University of Denver. He works extensively in coaching and speaking on the art of interpersonal communication in professional life—the nature of interpersonal communication that supports success in one's professional life.

He is or has been consultant and advisor to numerous federal agencies, including the Bureau of Health Professions, DHHS; the National Institute on Aging, PHS; the National Institute of Mental Health, NIH; the Administration on Aging, DHHS; and the U.S. Department of Education, Office of Special Education and Rehabilitative Services. He has also been an advisor to Congress; the U.S. House of Representatives Select Committee on Health; the House Sub-Committee on Health and Long-Term Care; the U.S. Senate Special Committee on Aging; the Senate Committee on Health, Education, Labor, and Pensions in the areas of health services delivery and disability issues; and the U.S. Senate Small Business Innovation Research Program. He is advisor to the Health Care Financing Administration, DHHS on health and mental health issues. He was also selected by the Bureau of Health Professions,

HRSA, DHHS to represent the field of aging on their Council on Disability Rehabilitation. Further, he is advisor to the Bureau of Health Professions, PHS; Health Careers Opportunity Program and advisor/panelist to the Office of Minority Health, PHS, DHHS, and the Division of Allied Health, BHP, HRSA, DHHS. He has been advisor to the World Health Organization on aging issues; advisor/panelist to the various grants programs of the Office of Special Education Programs (OSEP) of the Office of Special Education and Rehabilitative Services (OSERS); U.S. Department of Education as a member of their standing panel for 20 years prior to an additional three-year term including OSEP, NIDRR and RSA; was a member of the Scientific Merit Review Board of the Veterans Administration Health Services Research and Development Program; and is a current grants panelist for Health Resources and Services Administration, DHHS. He is currently advisor to the Smithsonian Institution in Washington, D.C. on behalf of their Accessibility Program for Children and Adults with Disabilities, and is narrator for the Smithsonian magazine. He is also currently an advisor/consultant for the American Institute for Research in Washington, D.C.

He is sought after as a speaker/presenter and has authored and presented over 600 presentations and workshops across the U.S., Canada, South America, and Europe on the art of interpersonal communication and persuasion in professional life.

His books include:

- *Hearing Impairment Among Aging Persons*, published by Sage Publications, Beverly Hills, California.
- *Rehabilitative Audiology: Part I—The Adult, and Part II—The Elderly Client*, published by Grune and Stratton, Inc., New York.
- *Communication Disorders In Aging*, published by Sage Publications, Beverly Hills, California.
- He was the invited author of the monograph entitled *The Communicatively Impaired Elderly*, for Seminars in Speech, Language and Hearing, Thieme-Stratton Pub. Co.
- *The Hearing Impaired Child In School* published by Grune and Stratton, New York.
- *Aural Rehabilitation: Serving Hearing Impaired Children and Adults* published by Singular Publishing Group, San Diego.
- *Aural Rehabilitation* published by Chapman-Hall Publishing Co., London.
- *Hearing in Aging* Singular Publishing Group.
- *Aural Rehabilitation—The Elements and Process For Serving Hearing Impaired Children and Adults* published by Thomson Publishing, New York, 2002.
- *Introduction to Aural Rehabilitation*, Plural Publishing, San Diego, 2010 and 2014.
- *Hearing and Aging*, Plural Publishing, 2014.

- *The Art of Communication*, Sound Wisdom Publishing with Jim Stovall, 2016.
- *The Art of Presentation*, Sound Wisdom Publishing with Jim Stovall, 2017.
- *The Art of Learning and Self-Development*, Sound Wisdom Publishing with Jim Stovall, 2017.
- *The Art of Influence*, Sound Wisdom Publishing with Jim Stovall, 2018.
- *Communication Disorders in Aging*, Plural Publishing, 2016.

Dr. Hull is the recipient of numerous honors and awards. He was elected Fellow of the American Speech-Language-Hearing Association. He was awarded the Red River Award by the Manitoba Ministry of Health and the Winnipeg League for the Hard of Hearing for significant service on behalf of hearing-impaired older adults. He was named the University Distinguished Scholar at the University of Northern Colorado. He was named Distinguished Pioneer in Gerontology by the Colorado Gerontological Society. He was awarded the Public Health Service Award, U.S. Public Health Service, PHS, DHSS for significant service to PHS, Region VIII for research and service on behalf of hearing-impaired older adults. He was also named Distinguished Scholar of the College of Health and Human Services, University of Northern Colorado. He was awarded the Faculty Achievement Award, College of Health and Human Sciences, University of Northern Colorado, for outstanding scholarly activity and teaching excellence. He is a recipient of the Award of Excellence for Outstanding Public Leadership in the Cause of Better Hearing and Speech. He was again named Distinguished Scholar of the College of Health and Human Sciences, University of Northern Colorado, and was awarded the Outstanding Faculty Achievement Award. He received the Distinguished Professor Award at Wichita State University by the University chapter of Mortar Board. He was also awarded the Wichita State University College of Education Teaching Award for Excellence in Teaching and the Emery Lindquist Faculty Award for Scholarship and Teaching. He was awarded the 2001 and the 2006 Professor Incentive Award from Wichita State University.

In 2002, 2003, 2004, 2005, and 2007 he was named to *Who's Who Among America's Educators*. In 2009, he received the President's Distinguished Service Award at Wichita State University. He received the Rodenberg Award for Excellence in Teaching by the Wichita State University College of Health Professions in 2014.

Dr. Hull was educated at McPherson College with a B.A. degree in Forensics, Drama, and Mass Communication; University of South Dakota with an M.A. in Communication and Communication Disorders; and the University of Denver, School of Communication with a PhD in Audiology/Neurosciences. He is an active member of the American Speech-Language-Hearing Association, the Academy of Rehabilitative Audiology, and the American Academy of Audiology, and holds ASHA Certification both in Audiology and Speech-Language Pathology. He is Fellow of both the American Speech-Language-Hearing Association and the American Academy of Audiology.